To Susan,
Thank you so much for
our goal of giving back!
home.
Jin
Drew

ANATOMY OF A MIRACLE

Drew's Story

A journey of hope, courage and faith

The unexpected journey of a young boy with a rare illness whose struggle to reclaim his health and recover will make you believe in miracles.

Jennifer M. D'Auteuil

WestBow
PRESS
A DIVISION OF THOMAS NELSON

ISBN: 978-1-4497-6087-8 (sc)
ISBN: 978-1-4497-6088-5 (hc)
ISBN: 978-1-4497-6086-1 (e)

Library of Congress Control Number: 2012913527

WestBow Press books may be ordered through booksellers or by contacting:

WestBow Press
A Division of Thomas Nelson
1663 Liberty Drive
Bloomington, IN 47403
www.westbowpress.com
1-(866) 928-1240

Because of the dynamic nature of the Internet, any web addresses or links contained in this book may have changed since publication and may no longer be valid. The views expressed in this work are solely those of the author and do not necessarily reflect the views of the publisher, and the publisher hereby disclaims any responsibility for them.

Any people depicted in stock imagery provided by Thinkstock are models, and such images are being used for illustrative purposes only.
Certain stock imagery © Thinkstock.

Back cover photos courtesy of Rick Lopez Photography.

Printed in the United States of America

WestBow Press rev. date: 8/21/2012

A Foreword by "Alli"

Starting out as a pediatric resident in 2005, I knew early on that I was destined for a career in pediatric hematology/oncology. I was drawn to the physiology of blood disorders and cancer, and I was unquestionably inspired to do further research in the field. I assumed that with such a career would undoubtedly come the substantial bonus of long-term interpersonal relationships with patients and families. However, until my second year of my hematology/oncology fellowship, I didn't entirely grasp the impact such a job would have on my learning, my life, and the lives of the families with whom I would come in contact.

I still remember meeting Drew, and his redheaded band of brothers, in the spring of 2009. While my senior mentors in medicine always said there would be families along the way that I would relate to on a personal level, I didn't quite believe it until I met this lovely (a word I don't generally use as it fits the too-good-to-be-true category, but that is a perfect descriptor) group of people. The D'Auteuils were naturally shaken by Drew's diagnosis of severe aplastic anemia. I can visibly recall sitting in a small conference room, with my Division Chief, Drew's Attending Physician at the time, and Drew's parents, drawing the presumed pathophysiology of this devastating illness on the board. Drew's mother Jen, a pediatric nurse practitioner, astoundingly assumed the role of "mother," placing her incredible body of knowledge and a lifetime of medical care on hold to digest the information. Pete, Drew's father, a pilot with no medical background, asked questions that astounded us in their complexity, graced by medical intuition. I remember sitting across from this couple of lovely (i.e., amazing) individuals and knew we would form a substantial bond.

And then there was Drew, an unassuming 10-year-old redhead, with the sage mind of a 20-year-old, and the guts and soul of a veteran. I could always tell that Drew's questions, well thought-out and intuitive, were only the pinnacle of additional questions, fears and brewing thoughts. I will never forget our conversation regarding bone marrow transplant; he wanted to discuss the mechanics behind how we, as physicians, intended to replace his bones with someone else's. Without hesitation, I assured him it was much more pleasant than envisioned, but we laughed and made a pact to discuss each new landmark with the same candor. And so, we continued on, myself and the D'Auteuils; it took me about six months to properly pronounce their last name (I can still see Pete mouthing: "D'Auteuil" like "Okay") but things settled out.

Drew underwent his bone marrow transplant, and we addressed each speed bump as it approached. Jen never ceased to amaze me with her email updates: full of accurate and precious information, and always tainted by the appropriate degree of humor. These emails were a valuable pipeline to Drew's ups and downs, both medically and emotionally, not to mention a monologue about clean countertops and the trials and tribulations of rectifying a wood-burning stove with bone marrow transplant precautions.

Drew's precipitous illness in the spring of 2010 served as a turning point in my training--I can picture day one in the Intensive Care Unit as though it were yesterday: Drew lying intubated, medically paralyzed, and the fear in his parents' eyes. I can still hear my internal monologue shouting *"no no no, not this child, not this family."* I handed over my cell phone number, opened the line to 24-7 communication, and visited daily. I had seen too many other children follow this path and knew that the course had the potential to be dismal. Jen and I sat down one afternoon and she asked if I had been raised Catholic. I had never associated my religious upbringing with my interpersonal approach, nor had it played a substantial role in my medical life, but over the next few days, as Drew started to slowly, one might say miraculously, improve with carefully thought-out but partial leap-in-faith medical therapeutics, I returned to that conversation in my mind.

Two years later, as an Attending Physician having completed my training, I still see the D'Auteuils in clinic on a regular basis. We joke about the weather, commiserate about "suicides" in lacrosse practice, and wonder over Drew's straight As in school. Drew recently joined the Jimmy Fund Clinic on a trip to Florida for Red Sox Spring Training. On his 20th tear down the water slide at our resort, I watched his grinning face emerge from the water, and couldn't help but think: "miracle."

Jen once sent me an email in the wake of his Intensive Care stay and rehabilitation, the last two lines of which were: "This has been a really tough year and having you on our side is an enormous comfort." I saved it in my "happy" folder. I'm fairly certain we, in medicine, and individuals in other professions, each have one of these folders, albeit not everyone will entitle it their "happy folder." Looking back on my training, I thought, "It had really been a tough three years, but thank goodness for the D'Auteuils." My figurative understanding of the interpersonal relationships intrinsic to a career in hematology/oncology did not prepare me for the enormous impact such a relationship would have on my career, and notwithstanding, the rest of my life. Over the past three years, I have witnessed the raw effect of the medical decisions we make on a daily basis and the precious and tenuous nature of health. I have watched one of the strongest families I have ever met battle back from adversity, and I have cultivated a fierce pride in Drew's courage. Drew is as healthy as he is today, yes, due to medical management, but undoubtedly due to the dedication of his family, their faith and persistence, and Drew's unfailing patience. My relationship with the D'Auteuils made me realize that it is ok, even beneficial, to *have* a relationship with families. That every bit that you learn of a patient and his or her family, is every bit more effort you dedicate to their care. When asked to write a forward to Jen's book, I accepted without hesitation. How else could I thank this family for their relationship, their trust, and their confidence in my care over the years? There is no doubt that I am a better doctor as a result.

Allison O'Neill, MD

Acknowledgements

Where do I begin? Thank you to our family and friends who helped us throughout this journey. Your love, loyalty and patience did not go unnoticed. Family ties and friendships are challenged by adversity and I thank all of you for standing by us. There are simply too many of you to name. You know who you are.

Thank you to Father Aggie and everyone at St. John Neumann's Parish for their prayers and kindness. We belong to a wonderful church community!

Thank you to everyone at Amherst Wilkins School, Amherst Middle School and Souhegan High School for their endless support of all three of our boys. We are forever grateful to you all.

Thank you to local organizations and businesses who supported us and helped Drew feel more like a normal kid like Cinemagic, Toadstool Bookstore, Halloween Annex and Pizza Hut of Merrimack.

Thank you to Make A Wish Foundation and their amazing wish grantors Kim Carmichael and Lynda Pearson. Your gift gave Drew something to look forward to and what a gift it was!

Thank you to Joe and Jennifer Andruzzi of the Joe Andruzzi Foundation, for all that they do for families affected by illness. Your foundation and friendship has been a great gift to us.

Thank you to Children's Hospital Boston and everyone there who took part in healing Drew; to the Jimmy Fund of the Dana Farber Cancer Institute. We were so blessed to live close to you and benefit from all that you have to offer. Thank you to Dr. David Williams, Drew's first defender and the one who first prepared us for this journey. Thank you to all the Jimmy Fund and Children's doctors including Dr. Christine Duncan, Dr. Leslie Lehman, Dr. Steve Margossian and Dr. Andrew Place. Thank you to Dr. Sally Vitalli and Dr Sung-Yun Pai and all the nurses and staff of the ICU for your expertise, skill and compassion during Drew's stay in the

ICU. Thank you Frannie Northgraves for being the wonderful nurse that you are. Thank you Brianna O'Connell for endless hours of fun you created for Drew. Thank you to everyone on 6W and 6E for your wonderful care of Drew. Thank you Erin and Robin (Jimmy Fund) for being such skilled and caring nurses. Thank you to everyone at Children's and the Jimmy Fund that we may have inadvertently omitted.

Thank you to the Core Medical Group. Your generosity during Drew's illness was so unexpected and yet so appreciated. We are forever indebted to you. Thank you to Jaiden's Angel Foundation - a wonderful foundation that helps families during crisis in honor of a beautiful little girl.

Thank you to Raytheon's Aviation Department and Dartmouth Hitchcock Manchester for the continued support and consideration that you have offered us over the last few years. Your patience and generosity allowed us to care for our son, with the security of knowing we would be welcomed back.

Thank you Amanda Benson. We welcomed you into our home at a time no one was allowed. Your gift of teaching and your friendship to our family will never be forgotten.

Thank you Kristen McTigue for helping me navigate the resources available to us and for being my friend.

Thank you to my fellow AA Moms. Together we have found strength, courage and amazing friendships across the country. Someday, we will all meet and celebrate our common bond and successes. I love you all!

Thank you Deb Barrios for being my friend, confidante and fellow "Mom-rade" in this war.

Thank you Jennifer Parkhurst for being Drew's first BMT cheerleader. Thank you Jennifer Thibeault for your ideas to support our family. Thank you Barbara and Steve Nelson for sharing your own experience and optimism.

Thank you to Aunty Dayna and Uncle John. My children were blessed with an extra set of grandparents. Thanks for sharing in our lives. Thank you Carri for being there always. You're more my sister than my friend.

Thank you to Dr. Allison O'Neill. By now, you truly must realize how much you mean to us. Words will never express the full extent of our gratitude. Your intelligence, patience and compassion make you the wonderful doctor that you are. We were privileged to have you on our side during this journey.

Thank you Poppa for encouraging me to share this story. You were right...it wasn't easy but I'm so happy I did it. I love you Pop.

I have to also thank Ginger for being our loyal protector and four legged member of our family. You kept Drew company, comforted him and watched over him in your own special way. For that, I am grateful to you always.

Thank you Steven Manro for being the considerate and caring person you are. You are an impressive example of selfless generosity. It's our hope that many others will follow your example and join the registry to give others the gift of life.

Thank you to all the men in my life: Pete, Kevin, Ryan and Drew. You all make my life complete and I love you all so much.

Thank you God. Thank you for miracles, for prayers answered and for the strength to write this story. May I never forget to believe and be grateful.

To Steven Manro.
Our hero.
Without your generous gift of life,
we wouldn't have such cause to celebrate.
Forever in your debt.

In Loving Memory
Of
Theresa Ann McGowan Murphy
The one who first taught me to believe.
I hope I made you proud.

I AM...

I am a funny and happy kid that has AA.
I wonder why my medicine tastes so disgusting.
I hear my dog barking at the neighbors.
I see a hippopotamus flying through the air on a unicycle.
I want to be healthy again.
I am a funny and happy kid who has AA.

I pretend to be a millionaire and buy a mansion.
I feel happy when I see my dog's face.
I touch her fur and snuggle her.
I worry if I am going to get better.
I cry when I see people being cruel to animals.
I am a funny and happy kid who has AA.

I understand there are a lot of kids with cancer.
I say it's just not fair.
I dream someday we'll find a cure.
I try to fight through it.
I hope others will win their battles.
I am a funny and happy kid who has AA.

Drew D'Auteuil, 10 years old
September 2009 school poem assignment

Introduction

I am not an evangelist. I am not a biblical scholar, nor do I have a degree in theology. I am a wife and a mother to three wonderful boys. This story is about how our lives changed course as a result of the illness of my youngest son. It's about the way we learned that our lives unfolded in a manner that had us unexpectedly prepared in more ways than we realized to take this journey. This story is about how faith can carry you through the hardest times of your life. This story is not told in an attempt to refute modern medicine or the brilliant minds who treated Drew. We were very fortunate to live close to one of the premiere children's hospitals in the world. His treatment was, without a doubt, of the highest quality given by some of the best nurses and doctors in practice today. We wouldn't be where we are today without them and we will forever be grateful.

This story is about gratitude...to God, our family, friends, church, school and community who supported us throughout this. Gratitude to the amazing doctors, nurses and staff that cared for Drew. Gratitude for the foundations and institutions that supported us as a family. Paying it back will take the rest of our lives. This story is about what we believe is a message to be told - a debt to be paid for which the reason is not yet understood.

This story is not written to encourage religious debate or defy the principles of nature and science. This is our story. This is Drew's journey. We just wanted to share it with you.

Prologue

It was May 31st of 2009 and I was walking our German Shepherd, Ginger. I usually liked to take her about three miles, sometimes longer. It was a beautiful day and late in the afternoon. I had the time to take Ginger for a walk and took advantage of it. My husband Peter and I have three boys. Twins Kevin and Ryan, 14 at the time, and Drew, who was then 10 years old. I worked part-time as a pediatric nurse practitioner, a position I loved, and Pete was working his dream job, flying for Raytheon. The previous weekend was Memorial Day weekend. We had spent it opening our pool, seeing friends and watching Drew play in a soccer tournament. Ryan was playing for the school baseball team and Kevin was on a travel lacrosse team. We were very busy, but very happy.

This particular day is one that has come back to me very often in the last few years. It was during that walk I found myself reflecting on how good our life was at that time. We had decided the week before to take advantage of the high school, practically located in our backyard, rather than send the twins to a private school in the next town. We had also decided to hold onto our six-year-old cars in lieu of new ones and the car payments that we would incur. We had taken a trip to Barbados during April vacation for a medical conference I attended and I had just put together a photo book and enlarged a favorite picture of the boys on a snorkeling tour we had taken. I remember thinking at the time how profound this feeling was and the sense of comfort and happiness that accompanied it. *We have a good life.* We certainly didn't have the biggest house or bank account in town, but we had everything we needed and more. I didn't realize it at the time, but I now look back and realize that I needed to recognize how blessed we were in order to handle what was about to come our way. I needed to know that I had a good life because I was about to realize how bad it could become.

Part I

Chapter 1
The Journey Begins

Pete and I were married on October 2, 1993. Before our first anniversary, we learned we were expecting. By my seventeenth week, we learned we were having twins. Our parents were ecstatic. We were happy but more than a little apprehensive. We were going to be brand new parents of twins! What a way to start. We were newlyweds, just starting out in our careers, trying to buy a house and now about to become new parents. My mother, at the time, had been battling a terminal form of brain cancer for about five months. As a nurse, I knew that her chances of survival were quite low, but I tried to focus on the time we had then and make the most of it. On March 5th, 1995, Kevin John and Ryan Edward were born and we couldn't have been happier. Fraternal twins, both redheads, each one unique and perfect in their own way. I prayed from the day they were born until their first birthday that my mother would live to attend their birthday party. She passed away peacefully two weeks later, my prayers answered.

Two years and nine months later, early in the morning of November 14th, 1998, Andrew Liam, or "Drew," was born. A third boy and a third redhead. His sweet disposition was obvious at birth. We liked to refer to him as the baby who was born smiling. To be more accurate, he first started to smile at four-and-a-half weeks, a milestone I documented with lots of pictures. Our family was complete and I couldn't see life being any better than this. I happily went through the stages and milestones of childhood and motherhood...long nights of feedings, spit up, diaper changes, pediatric appointments, playdates, potty training, first days of school, first communions and so on. During August of 2004, we brought Ginger home to become another member of the family. The boys' love of Ginger and her canine devotion to her family will be evident later on in this story.

Drew, 2 months old

Kevin and Ryan were typical boys. They loved planes, trains and automobiles. They loved Legos and Rescue Heroes. They played soccer, tee ball and eventually football and lacrosse. We put them on skis at age five and, in turn, Drew started to ski when he was four. In contrast, when Drew was introduced to dinosaurs at Kevin's and Ryan's kindergarten play, he was smitten. For every train, car and airplane the twins had, Drew had a dinosaur. His room was filled with dinosaur toys, books and decorations. He could spend hours playing with them. In addition to dinosaurs, he loved all living creatures from the sea to the jungle. Along with his brothers, Drew also tried tee ball and football, but eventually settled on soccer as his sport of choice. "Sweeper Drew" we called him, a reflection of the defensive position he played. He also had a special nickname, "Drewser the Bruiser," because he was such a big boy. By the fourth grade, he was the same size that his older brother Ryan had been in the sixth grade. Friends and family started to refer to him as "the Bruiser" regularly and he didn't seem to mind it at all. I never would have thought that a time would come when I would never again call him that nickname.

Drew obviously never had the opportunity to meet his maternal grandmother. Pete's parents had retired to Florida in 1999, and we visited them when we could. We were very lucky to have my father living close by, and "Aunty Dayna and Uncle John Preble" as well, my best friend Carri's parents who stepped up to be surrogate grandparents and treated our boys as if they were their own. Our boys have been truly blessed to have them in their lives. Carri was their aunt as much as our other brothers and their wives were.

Sweeper Drew   *Drew at a dinosaur museum, age 5*

There were three times during Drew's third year where he came to me to talk to me about "Nana." Three times he told me a different story that sounded like it was specifically about my mother. He told me once about how "Nana" had "fixed his bed because it was pretty broken." My mother did a lot of woodworking. Another time, Drew mentioned her love for lobster dinners. The last time he mentioned something about "Nana" was about the "boo-boo" she had in her head. (My mother had a brain tumor.) At the time, I loved to hear it and just accepted it as something he must have overheard us talking about, but there are times I wonder. Since he had obviously never met her, one time I asked him if he saw "Nana" in a family picture and he did indeed pick her out. I never questioned him about these few times because I knew enough about child development to know that he still lived in a fantasy land, so to speak, and kids will often respond with what they think *you* want them to say. I just took the three episodes at face value. He never spoke of her the same way again after his fourth birthday. It's always heartwarming to see or hear reminders of those you have lost. I had a small notebook that I liked to write down things that they boys had told me at various times and wanted to remember always, like when Ryan discovered a Japanese beetle and wondered how it got all the way to our house from Japan, or when Kevin announced he was going to build a rollercoaster in our backyard. Those are the memories you want to keep and treasure forever.

Drew and Ginger

Chapter 2

On June 1st, Drew came home from school and told me he had a rash. He was in the fourth grade at the time. As I was making dinner, I glanced at his arm saw a small area of a lightly speckled rash, and being the experienced pediatric practitioner that I am, dismissed it immediately and didn't give it another thought. The next evening, while I was putting him to bed, he adamantly demanded that I look at his rash again. This time it was different. He was now covered in that same speckled rash all over his body. Tiny red dots enveloped him and when I started to look him over more carefully, I found bright new bruises in areas where there shouldn't be, like behind his knees and on his chest and shoulders. Not the normal bruises that kids have all the time on their forearms and shins. This was a rash that could instill fear in the hearts of many a medical professional and I was no exception. I knew something was wrong. I had to wait until the next day, June 3rd to call his doctor. I called his primary care doctor's office first thing in the morning but couldn't get an appointment until 4:30 that afternoon. That day, Drew had "Field Day" at school, the annual day of outdoor activities and fun. I spent the day in a state of apprehension, thinking about post-streptococcal infection syndromes and other things I must have missed, and trying to calm myself that it would be ok. I constantly second-guessed my decision to send him to school.

After we picked up Drew from school, he did seem more tired than usual, but we assumed it was from field day. We brought him to his appointment and his PCP (Primary Care Provider) immediately ordered some lab work. It was with an awful feeling in my gut that I watched the nurse try to draw blood and when the first attempt failed, observed how the blood flowed down Drew's arm like it was water. Blood is thick...it doesn't roll down your arm like that! Immediately the clinician and mother in me started to clash, telling myself to stay calm and don't panic, while I also started thinking of possible diagnoses including ITP (idiopathic thrombocytopenia - a disorder that causes your platelets, the clotting part of your blood, to be low) and the big, scary one…leukemia. Now, I was frightened.

By 8:30 that night, I was beyond anxious. Just when I was about to lose it, I got the call from the doctor covering for Drew's PCP and was instructed to get to the ER immediately. Drew's platelets were critically low (platelets are the clotting factor in your blood). *I knew his blood shouldn't have run down his arm like that!* I had to wake Drew up and get him out of bed and into the car. Aunt Dayna came over to stay with the boys until she was relieved by Aunt Carri. It was all I could do to stay calm and avoid crying from fear in front of Drew. I didn't do a very good job of it. Once at the ER, an IV was finally started after multiple attempts and the doctors were making calls to see where to send Drew. Not only were his platelets low, but all his blood counts were low. They seemed to walk on eggshells around us and avoided answering our questions directly. Obviously, they couldn't, because they didn't know what was going on and telling us their suspicions wouldn't have done us any good in our present state. What they did tell us was that Drew was in a very dangerous condition. Because he complained of a headache earlier that day, they did a CAT scan, which led to concern that he might have a bleed in his head from a fall during field day. By 11:00 that night, we were on an ambulance heading to Children's Hospital Boston. We didn't know that it would shortly become our second home.

We were greeted at the ambulance bay by more scrubs and white coats than I had seen gathered at one time before. It was overwhelming; we were exhausted and scared. We sat in the rigid plastic chairs at Drew's bedside all night, praying in between counting ceiling tiles, while various doctors and nurses came in and out, until we were moved to a room on the sixth floor at about 7:00 AM. Drew was just begging us to let him sleep, he was so tired. That morning, Drew had a bone marrow biopsy. While I practically begged the doctor to tell me it was just ITP, he gently told me that it wasn't likely. We were looking at something much bigger. By Thursday afternoon, the doctors had their first sit-down with us and told us that they had ruled out most of the leukemias, but the doctor really felt that it was aplastic anemia or AA. I knew of only one patient in my clinic with this illness, and although at that time my knowledge of the illness was a little rusty, I knew that the treatment involved a bone marrow transplant. We spent our second sleepless night in his hospital room, waiting and waiting. Drew was transfused with the first of many bags of platelets. It was at this time that his nickname, "Drewser the Bruiser," became a painful irony of his condition. His lack of platelets caused the rash and multiple bruises. I've never been able to call him that since.

7

Friday afternoon, June 5th, 2009, Drew was officially diagnosed with severe aplastic anemia (SAA or AA). We were very fortunate to have Dr. David Williams, Chief of the Hematology Department and a prominent researcher, as Drew's primary doctor. At his side was a second-year fellow named Allison O'Neill, or "Alli," who would soon become our anchor at Children's Hospital and eventually, the Jimmy Fund, which is the Children's Cancer Center at Dana Farber Cancer Institute in Boston. She was also our first "angel" that we would meet on this journey. Drew didn't have cancer, but his treatment was the same for AA as many other childhood cancers. As we bit our lips and I tried unsuccessfully to hold back my tears, they told us about AA.

Aplastic Anemia strikes 1-2 people per million every year; less than half of those are children. It is a type of bone marrow failure and a "cousin" of leukemia. Bone marrow is the "factory" where your blood cells are manufactured. Your body needs white blood cells for protection against infection. Your red blood cells carry iron and oxygen, and your platelets help your blood to clot when you scratch or cut yourself. Drew's bone marrow was failing, leaving him vulnerable to infection, severe anemia and at a high risk for bleeding. That bone marrow failure left him bruised, easily fatigued and dangerously immunocompromised. Aplastic anemia is simply incompatible with life. Ninety percent of AA is acquired, which means you can look high and low, but you'll never find what caused it. It's widely believed that it's the result of a virus, which can be backed up by the fact that AA seems to appear in "clusters." These cluster cases appear around the same time of year, often in the same general area or region. A smaller percentage of AA is caused by rare hereditary conditions or external sources, like poisoning.

Dr. Williams was so patient and considerate and included the use of a white board to include drawings to try to show us what we were dealing with. I've always been more of a visual learner and despite my grief at the time, I remember focusing so intently on the drawings of cells and trying to listen at the same time. Drew was ruled out for any of the hereditary conditions and that caused Pete and I to drive ourselves to the brink of insanity wondering what we did to have caused this? Was it traveling? We were in Barbados just a few weeks before. Was it the annual carpenter ant treatment we had done to the house? Our environment had now become our enemy. We met Cassie, a nurse coordinator and educator who introduced us to the world of immunocompromised, or neutropenic precautions and isolation teaching, which was overwhelming and frightening. Neutrophils are white blood cells that act like the infantry in your immune system. They are the first line of defense against infection. Drew's ANC level (absolute neutrophil count) was near 0, so he had little defense against illness or infection. When your neutrophils were low, you were "neutropenic." Cassie even gave us a manual that we could refer to while we adapted to this new lifestyle, which included new ways to store food, cook and clean, and gave us our household restrictions necessary to keep Drew healthy.

Isolation living is a dramatic change for an active family like ours. No family, no friends, no visitors in our home. We worried what we would do if any of our appliances broke down? No service repair in our home? Drew could not go to public places. No raw food, no plants or flowers in the house and no animals either. Fortunately, we were allowed to keep Ginger. No more trips to help Aunty Dayna with the horses in the barn. We could no longer use dish or hand towels. Drew couldn't drink from the tap, eat deli meats or heat up leftovers. We had to wash all clothes daily and all utensils and dishes had to be run through the dishwasher. Paper towels, plates and cups became a way of life, despite feeling that we were single handedly bringing forth the demise of the environment. We even would have to adjust how we kept our woodstove burning as we weren't allowed to keep firewood in the house anymore because they often carried mold spores. We now kept our wood on the backdoor porch and Drew wasn't allowed to touch it. We also could no longer use the decorative screen on the stove front, but had to keep the unit closed to avoid releasing mold spores into the air.

Another irony in this illness and the chase for health is that the only food from outside our home deemed "safe" for Drew was deep fried fast food (deep frying kills everything) and uncut pizza. Pizza was allowed because it was usually baked in an oven in excess of 800 degrees. The pizza had to be uncut because the knife used may have also been used to cut raw vegetables or not cleaned to our new standards. Our local Pizza Hut eventually grew accustomed to our special orders for uncut pizza. No salad bars, buffet food, fountain drinks, soft-serve ice cream or slushies (I won't even mention what has been cultured on some of these spouts!). Not that we frequently had those items, but to be suddenly forbidden made them more desirable.

We were discharged on Saturday, June 6th and would plan on returning the following Tuesday and Friday to the CAT/CR (Center for Ambulatory Treatment and Clinic Research at Children's Hospital) on a regular basis to check blood counts while we waited the 2-3 weeks for the hereditary tests to be complete. Those illnesses had to be ruled out before any further plans could take place. We had been given strict instructions on what to watch out for, mainly symptoms of infection, the primary being a fever. Sunday morning, Drew seemed tired but he was smiling and happy to be home, apparently unaffected by his recent experience in the hospital. I asked him if he was OK and he just smiled at me. A short while later, I found him asleep in a chair in the living room. My gut on high alert, I checked his temperature and sure enough, he had a fever. That day we made our first panicked dash to the emergency room. As a former ER nurse, I know that every parent who arrives at the ER believes, rightly so, that his or her child is the most important and needs to be seen first. Unfortunately for us, Drew *was* the most high risk and did need to be seen first since he couldn't wait in a petri dish, I mean the waiting room, filled with sick people. Plus, with his nonexistent immune system, waiting could be the difference between life and death.

The first few times we had to go to the ER was beyond frustrating. Since AA is so rare, small community hospitals are not always familiar with it or accustomed to the severity of the immunosuppression that accompanies it and the special treatment these patients often needed. If we went to Children's in Boston, we had a bright orange card we just had to flash at the front desk and they would immediately whisk us out back. We used to call it our "Get into Jail Free" card. However, due to how immunosupressed Drew was, his doctors didn't want us to risk the hour-long ride to Boston and instead instructed us to go to the nearest hospital, have antibiotics started and then transported via ambulance to Children's. A very convenient blessing for us was that the ER director of our local hospital, Dr. Joe Leahy, lived in our town and he called me once he learned of Drew's illness. His own son was in school with Drew. He asked what our needs were and actually set up a protocol so that Pete and I could avoid the frustration of trying to explain time and time again why Drew needed to be seen immediately. Additionally, he saw to it that the particular antibiotic that Children's recommended was stocked just for Drew. That small gesture was huge in relieving some of our stress and frustration and we were so grateful. It seemed that at each obstacle we were facing, someone helped us find a way around it to the best of the ability available.

At this point, I had a hard time speaking to anyone, friends or family, and turned to texting as a replacement. The phone calls were too hard to take and it was brutal to try and repeat myself over and over again to concerned loved ones. I buried in myself taking care of Drew and avoiding any other contact. It was just too hard. Due to our medically induced isolation, avoiding people wasn't that hard either. Eventually, our friend and neighbor, Jay, researched and helped Pete set up a website so that we could communicate information to friends and family all at once. Drew's Caring Bridge site was set up that June. At first, I was completely opposed to it. Recognizing it and writing about Drew's illness meant that I had to accept it as happening and I wasn't ready to do that yet. It still felt like a nightmare from which I couldn't wake up.

Chapter 3

Wednesday, June 24, 2009 5:57 PM, EDT
A message from Jen.

Hi Everyone,

So far, I have let Pete handle most of the "public relations" regarding this latest development in our family. As you can tell, I still have trouble even saying the two words that Drew has been diagnosed with. It's not denial, just a defense mechanism. Truth be told, Pete has held me up for most of the last three weeks or I don't know how I would have survived. Although I still feel like I'm walking in a never-ending nightmare, I feel the stirrings of wanting to take control of this situation. So far, taking control means that my cleaning and "germ warfare" has been sent into warp speed. I think I bordered on obsessive-compulsive disorder (OCD) before. You should see me now.

I guess I really just wanted to thank everyone for everything. The prayers, well wishes, cleaning and paper supplies, gift cards, gas cards and inspirational cards. I don't think I'll ever be able to make everyone completely understand how much the support has helped me and our family. Driving to and from Boston so much has definitely taken its toll and the gas cards have helped tremendously.

I admit freely that I miss our old life. I was looking forward to a wonderful summer of hanging by the pool, going to the beach and seeing family and friends. Nowhere did I ever expect this turn in the road. It's very easy for me to be angry still about this or be jealous of others and their healthy families who still go about their lives. I still cry very often and unpredictably. I am learning to accept that we are not being punished. This is just a terrible illness that just happened to us. Drew is an innocent child and we were a happy family that were just the unfortunate recipients of this. I don't know how else to explain it and getting angry at God wouldn't have helped me at all.

To all my friends, I want to thank you for your perseverance in contacting me despite my lack of response. It's not that I didn't want to hear from or talk to you, it's just that talking is so hard. I'm working on it and hope to get in touch *with everyone before you all forget about me. Keep trying, I'm working on it. The fear of isolation has been very strong lately as well. It's even been tough to talk to my own family. I'm very grateful to all of you for your friendship.*

We have a difficult decision to make. I still don't know how to make such a decision but one has to be made. That at least isn't an option. The doctors continually tell us that there is a very real probability of a positive outcome but the two roads are riddled with real and potential obstacles and neither one is a "quick fix." All our research shows us that there are only two options.

I know that situations like these often lead people to pick a vice. Mine has been Sunkist soda. Those of you who have known me the longest know that once I kicked my Diet Coke habit more than 10 years ago, I don't drink soda. However, the first two weeks of this, I had a lot of trouble eating and Sunkist was the only thing that appealed to me. When my older brother came to visit us and I mentioned this to him, he asked me if I remembered that growing up, orange soda was the only soda my mother allowed us to drink when we were young. Apparently, I pulled some childhood memory out of the attic, dusted it off and embraced it. I guess it could have been worse.

I hope that you accept this for what it is. A statement, an apology, a request for your continued support and friendship. I have witnessed communities supporting families but never thought I would be on the receiving end and be so humbled by it. I admit it's a role that I would prefer not to be in. One thing is certain, we cannot fight this alone and we are so grateful for everything.

Thank you, thank you, thank you
Jen

That decision we needed to make was which course of treatment Drew would have. Drew had two treatment options; go directly to transplant or attempt immunosuppressive chemotherapy. If either of his brothers were a donor match, the transplant team advised going directly to transplant because a sibling match for bone marrow had a higher percentage of success than the immunosuppressant chemotherapy. Unfortunately, we learned soon enough that neither Kevin nor Ryan was a match for Drew. Another painful irony we learned is that they were for each other. During this phase, the doctors also took blood from Pete and me even though the chances of a parent being a match is really not likely. The only humor at the time we could draw from this was when Dr. Williams told Pete with confidence that despite his distinctly different coloring, the three redheads were indeed his. I used to tease Pete on occasion by reminding him that at least I knew they were mine. Gingers rule!

Once we eventually learned after those long three weeks that Drew did not have any of the hereditary illnesses, we decided to try the chemotherapy - a method of more fully suppressing his immune system in the hopes of encouraging it to start again. The doctors explained it as trying to make the bone marrow "wake up" and remember what it's supposed to be doing. The chemo agent was ATG or anti-thymocyte globulin. It is a serum made from horses that suppresses the T-cells in the body. Although AA isn't an autoimmune disorder, Drew's T-cells, which are another part of your white blood cells, were attacking his bone marrow and causing it to fail. The course of chemo was delivered by IV and took about five days. We then had to wait about 12 weeks to see if his system would respond. About 60% of kids respond to the chemo in varying degrees and of that 60%, about 30% would relapse at some point. The statistics didn't seem to be on our side, but there was approximately a 30% chance it would work and so we did the best we could to make an informed decision after spending quite a bit of time talking to Drew's team of doctors about it. They agreed and supported our decision to try the chemo first. It seemed to make sense, even if there was only about a 30% chance of cure. The doctors also said that a prolonged remission might also give science a chance to come up with more treatment options. After all, just over 30 years ago, no one survived this illness.

Drew had a PICC line (peripherally inserted central catheter) inserted for the chemo. This is an IV line that you can keep in up to several months so that he could avoid the constant needle sticks and IV starts. After the chemo was given, during the week of the 4th of July 2009, the plan again was for Drew to go home and return twice weekly to the CAT/CR for check ups and/or infusions if needed. That was the plan. We would return home and face the total isolation of the immunosuppressant lifestyle. It was sad to realize, eventually, that being in the hospital was less lonely than being at home. Between the changing shifts of doctors and nurses and Drew's care, it was always pretty busy there. Drew tolerated the ATG fairly well. A slight rash and some vomiting, but still that smile prevailed. Being allowed to stay in bed all day and watch TV? Even better.

For the first 11 weeks of Drew's illness, he ran nearly constant fevers that took over most of our summer. He was admitted to the hospital 14 times during that period to rule out sepsis, an infection that can take over your body. In between admissions, the longest period of time we were home was about 20 hours. Each time we were admitted, he had to have blood drawn, antibiotics were started, the fever would break and then it was a waiting game for 48-72 hours to see if any germs grew on culture. They never did. This was in addition to all the transfusions of red blood cells and platelets. Unfortunately, there is no way to transfuse white blood cells. Each time we arrived at the hospital, Drew hopped on the bed like he was in a hotel and happy to have a TV all to himself and would reach for the remote. Usually, Pete or I would have already grabbed it and knowing that they already cleaned the room, would be cleaning it again anyway. The staff came to know that we liked to keep a container of antibacterial wipes in the room with him. Drew was either the most resilient child or he actually didn't mind being at the hospital, despite the reason why. All the staff became familiar with his smile. Brianna O'Connell was the Child Life Specialist on the floor. She helped kids and families cope and adjust to hospital life and Drew came to adore her.

Drew and Brianna

During the short periods we were actually home, I carried out my new obsessive-compulsive cleaning to rid the house of any and all possible germs, both real and imagined, while Pete took a hacksaw to our sofa in our playroom in the finished basement that he was convinced was toxic. It was too big to take out except in pieces. If we could remove the offending issue, maybe the problem would go away? It didn't. The guilt was all-consuming. I thought about every morsel of food I fed my children, how I cooked it and what I served it on. Was there something in my well water? This was a nightmare and I wasn't waking up. Of course, there's a worse nightmare that a mother can realize but this was pretty bad.

Eventually, we would learn that a piece of popcorn stuck in his gums was the likely cause of the fevers, which stopped as soon as it came out. At first, the tiny piece of popcorn looked like an ulcer, which immunocompromised patients often have. Just when the doctors decided to have one of the dentists look at it, Drew happily showed me the offending kernel in his hand announcing that it had come out! The doctor on service at the time thought it might have been just enough to cause a mild septicemia and that's why Drew kept getting all those fevers. Drew had gone to the movies the Friday night before his illness. He was the king of oral hygiene in my house, often annoying his older brothers with his nightly ritual and all this time it was a piece of popcorn stuck in his gums? I guess I could see it since he hadn't been allowed to use anything other than a swab to brush his teeth. Freaking popcorn.

There is no way to describe my feelings during that time. Agonizing stress-induced insomnia, fueled by anxiety and the fact that most of Drew's admissions took place in the middle of the night. There were also our other two boys, just 14 years old and terribly worried about their little brother, who were trying to have a normal summer, most of which they spent at friends' houses. They were supposed to be having a great summer and getting ready for their first year of high school. Football was starting soon. We had to cancel our vacation plans. Our good friends across the street, the Curtises were so helpful in taking care of Ginger if we were gone. Several times, when we had to leave in the middle of the night, rather than wake the twins, their son Ben would come over and camp out in our family room so there was someone with the boys when they would wake up. We also came up with a system of placing a Christmas candle in one of our windows to signal that we had to leave during the night and to please take care of Ginger. It was these little things that helped ease some of that anxiety.

The previous posting was my first foray into writing on Drew's website. That "germ warfare" I referred to was indeed a war. No one could scrub the varnish off tables and banisters or the numbers and letters off remotes and keyboards the way I could. I should have bought stock in Lysol wipes. No doorknob, faucet, handle or light switch was safe and anything that fingers touched would be wiped down dozens of times a day. There was a time when I would clean everything over and over again all through the night. I couldn't sleep and was constantly checking on Drew and every time I'd try to go to back to bed, I'd think that I missed a spot somewhere, go back and do it all over again. It was an awful feeling and a likely justification for an admission to a psych ward. Keeping my house as germ-free as possible was the only thing I could control and I was obsessed. I also remember thinking throughout that time that I was never angry with God. I felt like I should be…I deserved to be, but I wasn't. Yes, I prayed obsessively too. Somewhere in my frazzled mind, I equated non-stop begging and pleading with God as more effective than just an efficient, organized and respectful plea for help. I pleaded for strength to handle this, grace to keep myself composed, and courage to face whatever was going to happen.

As his mother, avoiding kissing him on the face for fear of exposing him to some germ that might not have caused me any symptoms continued the strangulation of my heart. He seemed to always be covered in petechiae, the tiny red-dotted rash that heralded the arrival of AA. We also had to limit his physical activity for fear of injury. I would worry about him falling down the stairs or tripping on his way to the bathroom in the middle of the night. A blow to the head or torso could be life threatening so no bike, scooter, running or his favorite sport, soccer. We didn't drive him in the car unless it was to Children's. Drew was thrilled when Uncle John and Pete put up a rope swing he was allowed to use. During the brief time that he was home that summer, he was allowed to use the pool once his PICC line was out. I, of course, kept the chlorine levels relatively high. Ok, really high. I wasn't taking any chances.

Drew enjoying rope swing

Almost immediately, as word of Drew's illness spread, we were inundated with supplies like paper towels, antibacterial wipes, bottled water, paper plates/cups, plastic utensils and napkins. Several generous neighbors joined together in buying Drew an iPod iTouch to use in the hospital, something that proved to be a perfect gift for hospital living. In July, Kevin and Ryan held a music concert benefit for their little brother. They organized much of it themselves but had tons of help from school administrators who allowed use of the high school, their friends, a local band who donated their time, and many parents, teachers and our family. The local news even highlighted their concert on the nightly news along with a story about Drew. My department at Dartmouth Hitchcock held a blood and bone marrow drive. Bright orange wristbands with "Drew's Army" were being worn all over town - a reflection of community support and Drew's love of the Harry Potter series. We even had a picture of American Idol David Cook wearing one that he was given from someone in town. We were simply in awe of the support we were given. And that was only the beginning.

Chapter 4

Friday, August 7, 2009 11:41 AM, EDT

Happy Friday! It's another beautiful day. We hope everyone is able to enjoy it. Drew had a wonderful week with a few friends that stopped by during the hot afternoons and two easy appointments in Boston. To date, we believe that this is the first week that we have kept to the "regular" schedule that was assigned to us over two months ago. Lest we speak too soon, Drew's platelets are very low and unfortunately, we are starting to anticipate returning to Boston possibly sometime this weekend. However, the good part is it's been nine days since his last platelet transfusion and that's a nice stretch in between. All things considered, it's been a very good week.

We are still eager to hear positive news from his doctors but they keep reassuring us that it's simply too soon. Being patient is extremely difficult but we're trying each and every day.

Drew recently learned that he will not be starting school next month with his friends. Needless to say, he's very disappointed. However, we will be working with AMS to set up some kind of home schedule with him and are uncertain of the specifics but will be keeping him on track with his classmates. One of his teachers even offered to use a webcam for a class or two. We may even be asking some of his friends/classmates to walk to the house after school to bring his work to him and visit for a time. We hope and pray that this delay to his school year is quick and he's joining everyone soon.

Thanks again for checking in with us. Drew looks forward to seeing more of his friends in the coming two weeks and hopefully more beautiful weather.

Gratefully,
Team D'Auteuil

We did return for platelets that weekend. There are few things more frightening than watching your child bleed from the mouth and nose constantly. It's just awful. Drew's biggest problem seemed to be his platelets. They would drop quickly and he would bleed from everywhere, it seemed. He couldn't use a regular toothbrush. He had to use a swab to avoid bleeding and to protect his gums. A nick could be an open invitation to infection. The king of oral hygiene was even upset he couldn't use his floss. What kid complains about that? The physical effects of this illness were so traumatizing to us. To see him flash that famous smile of his with bloodstained teeth as he excitedly told me about a new book he was reading would only increase the chokehold already clutching my heart. His fatigue from the lack of oxygen carrying red blood cells made physical exertion, like climbing stairs, a chore. It seemed a hug from me would leave him bruised. I could tell, just by looking at him, at approximately what level his platelets were. A healthy, normal person's platelets range from 150,000 to 450,000 per microliter of blood. Drew often hovered in the 5,000-10,000 range. He would then need a transfusion in order to raise his level to a safer 60,000-90,000. However, within days, his level would nosedive and those were times I would bring him in, bruised, covered in petechiae and bleeding from the gums and nose and find that his level was only 3,000.

That summer, despite the fevers, hospitalizations, transfusions, lack of sleep and chronic anxiety, we tried to make the most of it. Friends and family could stop by, but no one was allowed in our house. Due to the high chlorine level I kept in the pool so that Drew could swim, I think everyone was definitely a little more blonde by the end of the summer. Coming to terms that this was real and that Drew would not be joining his peers for the start of fifth grade in a new school was particularly heartbreaking. It was also hard to try not to take the shine off the twins starting their first year of high school, but it was so difficult to get enthused. The school, particularly Drew's team of teachers and Maggie Kim, his guidance counselor, were so creative in coming up with plans to make allowances for him, like possibly holding outdoor classes, setting up wireless Skype in the classrooms, and planning to have the kids write cards to Drew. We also were told the school would provide a daily tutor for Drew so that he would stay in the same class year once he was allowed to return to school. We still had about eight weeks to see if the chemo would work and so far, there was no indication that it was. Drew never showed any signs of depression or anxiety. If anything, he almost seemed pleased to have me all to himself. This might have been his coping mechanism. In the early weeks, he occasionally would ask me hard questions, like, "is this illness fatal?" That was tough to hear and even tougher to answer, but he always seemed reassured when I told him that the doctors and nurses wouldn't let that happen and was smiling shortly thereafter, relieved and happy again despite his circumstance. I think he would have believed me if I told him his blood was now going to be purple. We would put him to bed, he would say his prayers and then curl up as usual and fall asleep. I was astonished at the emotional stamina of this child and he had no idea that I relied on his strength to help me stay strong. Keeping up the positive façade was exhausting but I would not let my son see me fall apart.

When Drew wasn't swimming that summer, I spent a lot of time out on our deck just praying and crying. This was when I wasn't cleaning the finish off something. All that cleaning wasn't burning up my stress calories. It was too hard to hear about other families enjoying their summers, going on trips and visiting fun places. I knew the jealously was wrong, but it was the way I felt. I avoided Facebook, something that had become quite popular in my town that year. We were given such an unfair sentence for no crime that we knew of. Drew was only ten years old. I also was figuring out that there was a distinct difference to feeling sorry for oneself and just being sad. It does you no good to beat yourself up for being sad. Everyone expresses his or her feelings differently and just as I wouldn't tell someone else how to feel, no one could tell me that I couldn't be sad. I could and I was. I was great at it.

Chapter 5

Good morning faithful members of Drew's Army. It's Tuesday September 1st. Hard to believe that once summer arrived just a few weeks ago with beautiful weather and now school's back in session.

For starters, we thought we would have some good news to share with you from yesterday. In a way we do, since there was no bad news. In summary, Drew woke last Wednesday looking like he was channeling the prom scene from the movie "Carrie". Fortunately, the episode last week conditioned us not to freak out and appearances can be deceiving because he was fine once he cleaned up, but we called the doctors and they wanted to see him that day rather than wait until Thursday.

The good news from that visit Wednesday was that his counts were stable from the previous visit and he didn't need to be transfused. That was very encouraging! The bleeding was probably the result of nicking a small area on his gum while brushing his teeth. The bad news was that it took four nurses and six IV attempts to get his blood drawn. The other good news was that Drew went all weekend without bleeding and we made it to the Monday appointment yesterday! We took this as a sign that maybe things were progressing and we would get some good news to report. That was not the case. There is no bad news either. Just more hurry up and wait. As Dr. Williams told us (again), we have been "unusually unlucky" in the course of Drew's illness and this sort of stretch of time would be considered typical. "Unusually unlucky" in medical-ese means Drew's course has "*($%^+" sucked "#%&*@()" in a major way. Still, maybe reaching a "typical" course is better than what we've experienced in the last 12 weeks (which still feel like years to us). Dr. Williams reiterated that the average rate of response to chemo is 96 days. That's 13.7 weeks for those of you reaching for the calculator. We are completing week nine post-chemo this coming Saturday. It's hard to be patient. Dr. Alli also reminded us that only about 30% of kids will reach a *complete remission by chemo. Please keep that in mind in your prayers for Drew. The next five weeks should be telling for us and the waiting is torturous.*

It's a gorgeous morning and the first day of school. The twins took off readily at least 15 minutes too early to go to their first day of HS and refused to let us take their picture. Time flies, as we can vividly remember putting them on the bus the first time for kindergarten. We are refusing to let Drew's home program depress us. After all, it's fifth grade. A blip on the radar of life. We have learned recently that another patient with AA is a 19-year-old-boy in Boston. He was diagnosed the fall of his senior year and missed that and his first year of college. We can deal with fifth grade. We look forward to seeing Mrs. Kim this afternoon and final preparations for Drew's tutoring. Drew also looks forward to our scheduling some of his friends to stop by after school daily.

In closing, we have a small request. If you have those piles of magazines/ periodicals ready to bring to the recycle bin at the transfer station, please let us know. The CAT/CR where Drew receives his outpatient therapy is lacking reading material for patients and families. We bring plenty of stuff for us and Drew to do, but we see many families who don't. They have some magazines but most of them are over a year old. If you would like to donate your magazines, please drop them off at our house or email us and we'll try and pick them up. **Please!! This is not a request for anyone to buy magazines! Only donate the ones you already have and were planning to recycle!**

Thank you again for prayers and support. We truly believe that good news is around the corner and wait for the day to share it with everyone.

Have a wonderful week!

Gratefully,
Team D'Auteuil

Our summer was filled with multiple trips to Boston several times a week. We developed a sort of routine. We would leave the house by 6:15 AM at the latest to be at the CAT/CR for 7:30 AM. We would have our stash of masks for Drew, hand wipes, hand sanitizer and what would become a regular passenger in our car, the pink bucket. I would also pack a specially prepared breakfast for Drew, usually his favorite Cheerios. Drew's medications made him ill nearly every morning and either in the car or shortly after arriving at the CAT/CR, he would vomit. Most of the time, Frannie would be his nurse, the second angel on earth we would be privileged to know. As a "seasoned" nurse myself, I was impressed with this young, fresh-out-of-school nurse's ability to connect with Drew, her technical skill, and her compassion. She was a welcome sight to us every time we saw her there. Not that the other nurses weren't wonderful as well. We never had any complaints. Frannie just had a great way with Drew and we were very thankful. She seemed to coax veins out of hiding and made him laugh despite his discomfort. His PICC line had been short-lived a few weeks before because of fear of infection, so he needed to be stuck every time we came in. If we kept to a regular schedule, we were at the CAT/CR on Tuesdays and Fridays. We usually ended up with an extra day in there somewhere because of bleeding issues. The episode I referred to in the previous posting was quite frightening. On that evening in particular, I had to drive Drew to Boston because he started vomiting blood, but when it continued in the car just after we left the house, I had to divert to a local ER. That experience alone aged me quite a bit. Fortunately, we were transferred to Boston, Drew was given his bag of platelets and we were home the next day. I was getting used to not sleeping.

Something that did me some good that summer was getting in contact with the parents of another boy affected by AA. Since hospital confidentiality laws prohibit staff from releasing personal information, Frannie, Drew's favorite nurse in the CAT/CR, talked to the other family and asked if they would be interested in speaking to us and they gave their permission to give some contact information. We started off talking via email and eventually would meet Adam and his family later on in our journey. It wasn't about misery loving company…it just helped not to feel so alone.

The school year had started and I couldn't make myself feel that familiar return of fall feeling, my favorite time of the year. It was too different. Drew started fifth grade at home, tutored by a wonderful teacher named Amanda. She would be another angel on earth that was sent our way by circumstance. She had an immediate connection with Drew; she appreciated his sensitivity, intellect and relentless sense of humor. She made school fun despite his confinement. His academic team and guidance counselors did as much as they could to include Drew in outdoor lessons and activities that he could participate in. They were able to get Skype installed so he could watch some lessons. It wasn't the same, but it helped. We would take long walks and meet Mr. Lambrou with his gym class outside in the school field and hear a chorus of "hi Drew!" from all the kids. Drew would often bring his new camera, a gift from our family friend Tom Neary, to document the many walks that we would go on to take up some time. A local company, the Core Medical Group, "adopted" Drew as a cause and sent us a gift basket that was filled with toys, gift cards, a Patriots blanket and so many other gifts! The timing was so impeccable because the basket was delivered one evening as I waited for a septic company to arrive because our system had started to back up that evening. Fortunately, the back up was only water from the washing machine because I noticed it early. What was also fortunate was that the employee didn't have to come inside the house. After he arrived, I learned quickly that the cause of the backup was multiple wrappers from granola bars that Kevin and Ryan had been flushing so that I wouldn't see they were eating them when they were supposed to be reserved for school snacks. Wonderful. A nice slap in the face of reality amidst my emotional pain. Teenagers. Just wait until they got home from their football pasta party. However, the arrival of the gift basket helped me redirect my frustration to gratitude and, in all likelihood, softened my response to this poorly timed household problem and poor teenage judgment. It would be easier to fix this problem than the bigger one looming over our heads. I had to move on.

We continued our weekly treks to Children's, each time renewed with hope and anticipation, only to be disappointed to hear again that Drew's bone marrow wasn't responding. We were still in waiting mode and the longer it went on, the more our hope dwindled. We tried to keep autumn as normal as possible and we were allowed to take Drew apple picking, except that he couldn't eat the apples and had to wear gloves. Aunty Dayna and Uncle John came along to buy the boys their Halloween pumpkins. Drew also missed climbing in the trees, but I'm pretty sure they aren't supposed to be doing that anyway.

Kevin, Drew & Ryan applepicking wearing Drew's wristbands

Aunty Dayna and Drew

By late September, with still no bone marrow response to the chemo, the search for a compatible donor became more focused. Dr. Williams and Alli reassured us that a transplant can be postponed right until the last minute should his marrow suddenly respond. The end of the 12 week timeframe for marrow response was closing in on us and you didn't have to be a genius to figure out that Drew would likely get his transplant around his birthday (Nov 14th) and then probably spend the holidays in the hospital. By mid-October, Dr. Williams encouraged us to "psychologically prepare" ourselves for Drew to have a transplant. I didn't know what that meant other than to accept the inevitable. The chemo didn't work and Drew would have to have a transplant.

Chapter 6

Thursday, October 1, 2009 5:09 PM, EDT

COPING MECHANISMS: *When faced with a stressful or anxiety-producing situation, we resort to a number of coping mechanisms to help us process and manage it effectively...or you get together with a whole bunch of great people and have fun! We have learned recently that there is a night at Hampshire Hills on October 16th planned (adults only) and we are hoping to be able to join you there. For more information, please contact Jen Thibeault. We again find ourselves in a humbling position to thank those who have supported us in so many ways. Jen T., you have proven yourself to be a great friend and we are forever grateful.*

We have our meeting with the transplant team on October 13th and had hoped that perhaps this event could be a celebration of sorts. Now, we are going to try and view it as a "pep rally" to help us gain some more momentum for the coming challenges ahead of us. We have a deep faith, but have never seen ourselves as evangelical. However, we believe at this time that although our prayers haven't been answered in the way that we hoped, we have to believe that He will help us navigate through the bumpy road ahead. We have no other option but to believe, not only for ourselves, but for a little boy who just wants to be back in school, playing soccer and hanging out with his friends. We don't believe that God sends us challenges. He helps us with the challenges that we find ourselves facing. You could view Him as another coping mechanism and that is exactly what we are doing.

Thank you again for all your prayers. Thank you to friends who insist on calling and coming by even when we're in "lock down." We appreciate everything you do. We hope to see you on the 16th.

In appreciation,
Team D'Auteuil

On October 16th, an amazing event took place. A benefit night was held for us at a local health club. Pete and I were able to stop by for a couple hours, stressful as it was to leave Drew home alone with only his brothers. We hadn't left him alone at all since his diagnosis. He was simply too fragile. Jennifer Thibeault organized this event for us. Jen and I had known each other since 8th grade, but hadn't seen each other or spoken in over 23 years, just due to life's different roads. During the spring, Drew had been talking about his new friend Zach who lived up the street and as it turned out, he was her son! At the benefit she organized, we were overwhelmed at the attendance, the volunteers, the support of local businesses and the outpouring of generosity that was displayed. It was the first time we had seen so many friends since coming under house arrest. It was hard to relax and have fun, but we did manage for a little bit. A wonderful local photographer and friend, Rick Lopez, took a photo journal of the night and donated the photos to us. It's a great keepsake that I still look at from time to time and again, feel so grateful. I can look back at those pictures now and smile at the memory and the strength I gained from knowing so many were praying and pulling for Drew.

This night was wonderful, but also hard. I remember crying the whole way home, humbled by the support we had but also burdened by the reason why we had this support. Our son was ill, very ill, and needed a very risky treatment. The combination of gratitude and grief was depleting the remains of what little sanity I had left. I learned early on, when I needed to cry, I had to cry. I didn't care who I cried in front of either. The doctors and nurses were used to my tears by now and never seemed less than empathetic or understanding. My son was sick. I was entitled to cry. Holding it in (as I did around Drew all the time) wasn't helping me at all.

Chapter 7

Wednesday, October 14, 2009 12:49 PM, EDT

RUNNING IN PLACE: Although, it feels like we are running in place this past week we have some good news. An excellent match has been found for Drew and the request has gone out to the local donor center and a date for admission has been scheduled for November 10th. Please keep positive thoughts and prayers coming that this donor agrees to donation and is in good health. We didn't realize it would be so quick to get the wheels in motion as everything so far has been "hurry up and wait." We do know that many families wait much longer for a matched donor so while we are very grateful, our emotions are a mixture of sadness, fear and also some stirrings of resilience.

Every day we thank God for our family, friends, community support, Children's Hospital and all the doctors working to cure our son.

Thank you,
Team D'Auteuil

The next couple of weeks were spent touring the transplant unit, meeting the various doctors who would be involved in his care and learning about the medications and treatment that he would be given. We signed the consent form the Friday before his admission with Dr. Christy Duncan and Alli. The process was long and we were warned it would be difficult because it would list virtually every side effect and complication imaginable. Somehow we got through it, signed it and felt the anticipation of changes ahead of us and some reluctant acceptance.

We had some good friends who had helped prep us for our journey, Barbara and Steve Nelson. We had met in town as football parents about eight years before. Just after they moved here and before we had a chance to meet them, Steve had developed a combination illness of aplastic anemia and myelodysplasia (a precursor to leukemia) and had a bone marrow transplant (BMT) at Brigham & Women's about 10 years before and was also a patient of Dana Farber Cancer Institute. Barb had told me all about Steve's illness years before Drew was diagnosed. To hear Steve confide in us about his time in the hospital and reassure us that Drew was going to be OK was encouraging to us. Here was walking proof. Although technically Drew would be treated at Children's, he was a patient of the Jimmy Fund at the Dana Farber Cancer Institute - the same place Steve had his treatment. Barbara was one of my greatest supporters just because she *knew*. She knew what we were about to embark on and even if it had been her husband and not her child, she had experienced the journey just the same. She knew all about isolation living and had some great advice about time in the hospital and at home. Just as this illness has been one waiting phase after another, the thought of fast forwarding to Drew's ten-year milestone was too much to visualize at the time. To think of Steve gave me more hope that one day we'd be the ones supporting someone else about to take the same journey, and that energized me a little.

Drew had spent some time alone during one of his visits at the CAT/CR with Alli talking to her about the transplant and what to expect. He knew that he would not feel good and that he'd lose his hair. He knew that he'd be spending his 11th birthday and Thanksgiving in the hospital and probably Christmas, too. I think he was taking it better than we were. I was so proud of him for talking to Alli by himself. He wasn't quite 11 years old, but I saw how he needed to also absorb and deal with this in his own way. I was very proud of him that day.

In preparation for the inevitable, Drew got his hair cut short in a funky style that allowed him to make a mohawk and we bought some dye for him to have fun with. Ross, the barber, had been cutting Drew's hair since he was three years old. We discovered, after bringing the boys to his shop for a while, that he actually lived just up the street from us. Several times during our isolation, on his way home from work, Ross would stop at the house and cut Drew's hair on the screen porch. We couldn't bring him to his shop and the fact that he lived so close was unbelievably convenient. Knowing Ross, I think he would have made the house call even if he didn't live so close, but it was an added bonus and helped me feel less guilty about asking for this special service.

On October 31st, Drew spent the morning going to the movies, courtesy of a local Cinemagic, with his friend Zach. They were allowed to watch a movie in a theater by themselves, with just me and Zach's mom, Jen. You should have seen us cleaning the armrests of the chairs, keeping a 10-seat

Drew's pre-admission haircut

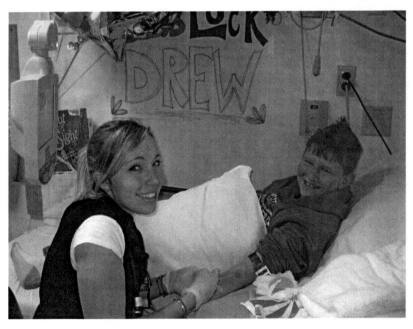

Nurse Frannie & Drew at CAT/CR

radius cleaned from all angles. Our local Halloween Annex seasonal store allowed Drew in before store hours to shop for a Halloween costume. That night, Drew went to "Halloween in the Village," an annual tradition in our town, for trick or treating. His platelets and red blood cells were low and he was quite tired after just an hour, but he was happy to be able to go. We also were allowed by local bookstore, "The Toadstool," and our local Barnes & Noble, to go in after store hours for Drew to "shop" for books to take with him to the hospital. We were so grateful to these managers that gave a small allowance for Drew to feel a little bit connected to the outside world again, even if the store was empty. It seemed every favor we asked of these businesses was given to Drew, and we were so grateful and humbled. There is good in the world. Despite his situation and knowing what was coming soon, Drew still continued to smile. It was like he knew something I didn't or may he just had barely enough developmental maturity to *not* understand what was happening and that, in turn, kept him smiling regardless.

Drew & Zach at their private movie showing courtesy of Cinemagic.

Drew's admission date was actually changed to November 12th, but we kept that to ourselves - a selfish act to spend two days with all our boys and celebrate Drew's birthday before his admission on the 12th. The

11ᵗʰ was Veterans Day, so the twins were home from school and we just spent it together as a family. We had a small birthday celebration for Drew that evening. No one really knew we were still home. Despite our growing apprehension, Drew's ever-present smile gave us fuel to hope and for holding it together. My father, or "Poppa," came over to see Drew on the 13ᵗʰ before we left for the hospital. He asked Drew what he was going to remember while he was in the hospital. At first, Drew answered "I'm Irish" with a smile. Then, after Poppa laughed, when he asked him again, Drew responded "I'll never give up." On the morning of November 12ᵗʰ, 2009, suitcase packed with new comfortable pajamas, robe, slippers and plenty of books and movies, we made our entrance on 6W at Children's Hospital.

Chapter 8

Saturday, November 14, 2009 3:47 PM, EST

Day 3: Today is the third day of chemo and Drew is starting to feel some effects. He's taking a nap right now after talking on Skype to his buddy Will. Anyone who has Skype, Drew's address is "sweeper drew." Later on, we hope to talk to his brothers via skype as well. His favorite nurse from the CAT/CR, Frannie came up earlier to see him for his birthday and the nurses came in a little while ago to sing "Happy Birthday." He got a birthday crown, balloons, an ice cream sundae and a Lego racer! The staff from 6E brought Drew a Wally the Big Green Monster for him all dressed up in Red Sox garb!

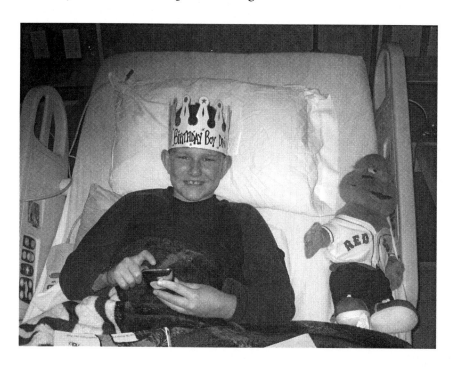

For this entry, we thought we'd just back up and tell you a little about where we are right now. Drew was officially started on chemo Thursday night. We are on 6W at Boston Children's hospital. After you go through the airlock double doors, you realize you're not in Kansas anymore. The unit is very bright and colorful and the common theme seems to be fish. Upon arrival, we were told that Drew's room was the "suite." As luck would have it, it is the largest room on the unit and it was available. There's plenty of room for us and Drew and he has 2 small dressers, a full daybed, refrigerator, desk, computer, TV, DVD and playstation. Drew's favorite thing about the room is that the ceiling has these really cool lights that have about 15 different settings and colors that he can control. We have decorated his walls with the many birthday cards that everyone has sent. We also have a calendar up to mark off each day that passes as one day closer to discharge. We also put up a family picture so Drew doesn't forget his two older brothers and a couple of photos of the special girl in Drew's life...Ginger. When we arrived, there were already many birthday cards waiting for him and a box from Core Medical Group with the most awesome Patriots hat and shirt with #11 and "D'Auteuil" on the back. He loved it! Thank you!!

Today is also special to us because it's Drew's birthday. We were able to spend a little family time on Wednesday with his brothers to celebrate. He's now officially 11 years old. Today is day -5 on the countdown to day 0, which will be transplant day, or Drew's new "extra" birthday next week. Drew has one day left of chemo and then radiation starts on Monday.

Yesterday we got to meet Adam. He was diagnosed with AA last September and had his transplant in April. Although he couldn't go in Drew's room, he was able to greet him from the hallway and say hello. We were able to talk to Adam and his Dad in the visitors' room and it was great to meet him and see him looking great and sounding so positive. It was really helpful to us.

Drew has had two visitors from the Hole in the Wall Gang group and yesterday played "Lacrossketball" with Jared. Jared taught Drew how to make a wallet from duct tape the day before. Apparently, he's a duct-tape artist. It's pretty cool.

We understand that the next several days may be difficult for Drew. We will try and update as we can. Thank you for keeping us in your thoughts and prayers. We definitely are in the right place for this and mark off each day on the calendar as another step in the right direction.

One last note: the Patriots are playing the Colts tomorrow night and Drew's hematologist, Dr. Williams, is from Indiana. He might be stopping by. We will have to plan to have Drew with his new hat and shirt on in addition to his Patriots slippers and blanket on his bed!

Thank you!
Team D'Auteuil

When we saw the #11 on the Patriots shirt, we were thrilled because Drew had met Julian Edelman a few months before during one of his admissions and that was his number! But back to business. Drew had four days of chemotherapy and that overlapped with four days of radiation. Drew spent his birthday vomiting or sleeping. During the time he would nap, I would huddle on my parent bed and cry. Leaving him alone in the radiation room and only being able to watch him through a closed circuit TV was agonizing. I wanted to be in there, to hold his hand and tell him how much I loved him and how strong he was. Instead, my little man would sing songs like "Kung Fu Fighting" to make us laugh. The strength of a mother must never be underestimated, but neither should her pain. There is little worse in this life than watching your child suffer. The questions I had asked myself over and over again nearly six months ago came back to haunt me. Why, why, why?? Why Drew? Why us? There was no answer that I received. I had to accept that this was happening and believe that Drew would not be supported by the doctors and nurses alone.

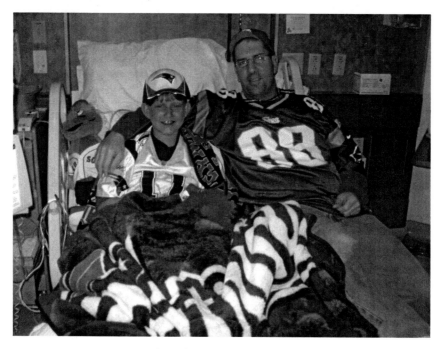

Drew and Dad ready to watch the big game!

Chapter 9

DAY 1: Yesterday was day 0. In our new welcome photo, you can see Drew pushing the start button on his transplant last night about 7 PM. The staff made him a big "Happy Transplant Day" sign to hang on his door and he also got a cake. The transplant was done by about 1 AM this morning. Although there was no problem with the transplant itself, the last-day-of-radiation side effects kicked in along with the prep work of preparing Drew with hydration, multiple other meds and ultimately it led to one of his toughest nights to date. He was up briefly this morning and is now very comfortable and napping. You can also see by the photo that he still has that beautiful head of hair. Its days are numbered though. Drew has actually mentioned a couple times that he wishes it would hurry up so he can be done with it and it will then grow back. His strength is amazing.

Now we begin the waiting process, something that this illness has forced us to face several times before. Today is day 1. Signs of engraftment (meaning the transplant is working) take about 3-5 weeks. The first 100 days are the most telling about how successful it will be. In the meantime, we hope for a boring hospital stay without any signs or symptoms of rejection. We will also be praying for no infection, as Drew is the most immunocompromised he's ever been. We have been told that the average hospital stay is about 4-6 weeks without complications. If there are complications, then we will be taking up residence at the Ronald McDonald House. For now, we plan on being here through Christmas.

Drew continues to receive mail on a daily basis and looks forward to it. Yesterday he received a big card from our parish, St. John Neumann, and it's proudly displayed next to the card from AMS and all the other cards sent to him. His room is getting more colorful by the day. Thank you!

You can check out a few new photos added, including one of Drew with Alli, his primary who has been with us from the beginning. We hope to add some more later on, so stay tuned.

In the meantime, please keep the prayers coming. Although we don't feel like we can fully relax until Drew is running on the soccer field and has joined his friends at school, we have some planned incremental stages of relaxation and the first one will be to see the signs of engraftment and be on our way home.

Thank you!
Team D'Auteuil

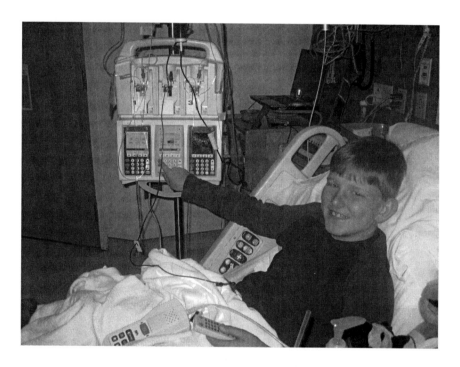

Pete and I had come up with a plan of rotating our time at the hospital so that we could also see the twins and keep them somewhat balanced, even if only with one parent at a time. We would rotate 24-hour shifts with Drew. I hated leaving him at all, even for just an hour but I knew that we had to do this. It was the only way that made sense for our family. Drew, still heavily medicated and feeling the effects of his treatment, would watch movies or cartoons when he wasn't sleeping. When he was awake, he was often sick and tired, despite the medications designed to keep him comfortable. We had to help him to the bathroom and that wasn't easy with all the tubes and wires he was attached to. Despite all this, he still found time to smile at us.

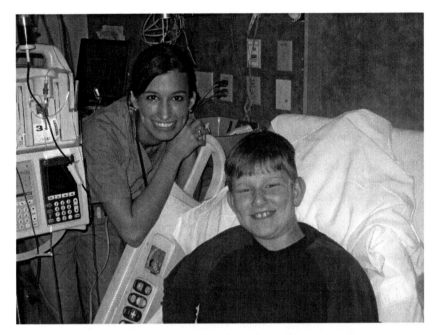

Dr. Alli and Drew on his transplant day November 18, 2009

The staff was considerate, compassionate and accommodating. Eventually, Pete and I would call each other just before arriving so that we could just meet at the drop off in front of the hospital to avoid paying parking fees. We also had to plan carefully and leave the hospital before 3 PM or it would mean we would have to wait until after 7 PM, otherwise Boston traffic would be awful. Drew didn't like it very much. He wanted us both there but we had to make some concessions. It also meant that we didn't see each other except when one of us would arrive and the other would hop in the car to go home. We didn't eat in the room anymore because the smell bothered Drew. Truthfully, I wasn't eating much anyway. I ate enough to sustain myself. Sleep was now officially a thing of the past. I just couldn't. In addition to being afraid of missing some sign or symptom, each time I woke and had to realize that this nightmare was still ongoing, was too tough to take. I stayed up most nights watching Hulu on the laptop computer that was provided for us, watching reruns of "King of Queens," "Seinfeld" and became a new fan of "Dexter."

The twins were doing OK, but I think they were struggling with worry about their little brother and the disruption of our former stability. They were sick of sleeping over at friends' houses, which was the primary reason for Pete and I to develop the shift rotation at the hospital. We wanted the twins home in their own beds. Their academic team was keeping a close eye on them and helping them stay focused. Although they were freshman players, their football "brothers" kept stickers with the initials of "DD" on their helmets in honor of Drew and their coach recognized them as the great big brothers they were at the end of their varsity championship season. We missed most of the games, along with teacher conferences, parent coffees and just adapting to a new high school environment. I now lived in sweats and we washed Drew's clothes every day, either taking them home to wash or using the washer and dryer provided for us on the floor. This was our new way of life and we had no idea how long this would last. We had to wait until the doctors had proof of Drew's transplanted marrow finding its way to the right spot and begin working.

Kevin, Coach Beliveau and Ryan

During one of my long nights on the laptop and Googling endless information on AA, I came across another boy, Noah Ramos, in California, who was Drew's age and also had AA. I contacted his mom, Alaina Palomino, through his website and that contact led me to another mom in California, Jennifer Barrios and her son Ethan. Between these two moms, we started email correspondence that allowed us to vent when we needed to and applaud each other's successes. In particular, Ethan's mom Jen and I became quite close - as close as two people can get via email and when we share so much of the same journey. Ethan's transplant was eight days before Drew's and that timing was what cemented our friendship on this journey. We would compare notes, meds, and whatever was going on at that time. We also had our good friends, the Strattons, to lean on for strength, as their daughter Caroline waged a fierce battle against brain cancer. Until you've been in the position of having a truly sick child, you cannot appreciate the friendship and support that comes from those who know.

Chapter 10

Saturday, November 28, 2009 6:03 PM, EST

LEAPS & BOUNDS: *What a difference a day makes! The last four days have been exponentially improving for Drew and today is no exception. Drew's nausea and vomiting seems to fading steadily and today he's even eating! Bagel bites were the request of the day. That was the influence of Aunt Donna who told Drew that they were the only things she kept down while going through chemo. The staff emphasizes that they don't care where he gets his calories right now. He even had a "Sundae on Saturday" today.*

Drew has been officially declared a "boring" patient and that's what we love to hear. Even though the nausea and vomiting seem to be resolving, the throat/ mouth sores that usually occur have not showed up yet and although they still could, their duration will be limited since Drew's so far past his treatment and so much closer to producing healthy white blood cells. Now, all hope and prayers go toward keeping Drew healthy without infection and that he shows no evidence of rejection. We also hope that our biggest challenge facing us will be keeping him entertained in this room and unit for the next several weeks. Currently, we are pretty well stocked with games, books and even some school work.

We have felt some great relief seeing Drew acting like his old self. He is sleeping great, waking up and wanting to get out of bed and today he and Dad figured out that it takes 17 laps in the hallway to equal one mile. Drew's arms show no evidence of the previous battle zone from multiple IV sticks. He definitely appreciates the central line that is on his chest. (You were sooooo right Mr. Nelson!)

The only "negative" news to report is that the hair does finally seem to be admitting defeat. We have been expecting it and accept it as a necessary evil. Drew also can tell you quite clearly that it's temporary. Another 4-6 weeks and his scalp should be covered again, hopefully with the same red hair that we all know and love. There is a chance the color or texture could be different. My money is on the red. It seems like a strong color in my family.

So, in closing, thank you all again for keeping in touch. Your mail, comments and prayers are so helpful to us all. Please remember to keep our friends Caroline and Noah in your prayers as well.

Here's hoping for more positive updates!

Team D'Auteuil

P.S. Forgot to mention to check out the pics of the clowns. They have been a favorite of ours at Children's and the other day they had Drew laughing his head off as you can see by the picture!!

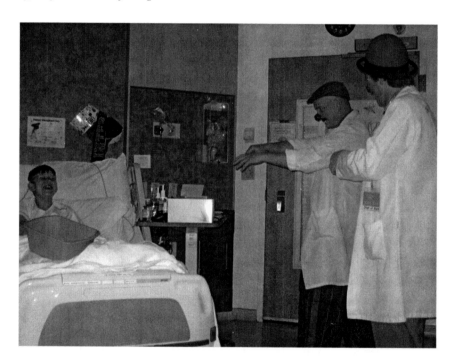

The days crept by slowly and we did all we could to keep Drew busy. In addition to the daily walks they encouraged, mask and IV pole included, Drew could spend time in the playroom when it wasn't occupied and took up painting some Christmas presents and pictures for family and also the staff. We played a lot of games and Drew also did a lot of reading. We kept in close touch with my brother Chris and his wife, Donna, who was then facing a battle with breast cancer. Donna is Drew's godmother. Over the phone, they bonded while sharing their chemo experiences.

Thanksgiving was quiet in the hospital for us. My brother John took the twins over to his house to eat and I had the hospital Thanksgiving dinner. I was trying to be grateful that Drew was doing well, but spending the holidays in the hospital was pretty depressing. The thought of spending Christmas here was too much to think about at the time. I kept up my email correspondence with Jen Barrios and in effect, we both cried on each other's shoulders. I was thankful that Drew's room had the computer access for me. Even though I also knew that Drew would lose his hair, it still hit me hard. Just before he lost it, Flashes of Hope photographers came in to the unit to photograph any of the kids who wanted some beautiful portraits taken. I treasure those photos. It was the last time that Drew looked like "himself" before the physical change of treatment took place.

The other exciting news that was taking place in our hometown was the "Crew for Drew" event. This awesome event, again organized by Jen Thibeault, was generously assisted by Michele Hennas and her staff from her salon "Hairthurium," who volunteered their time and talent to give crew cuts to anyone who wanted to show Drew support. Drew and I watched it play out in photos of that evening and again, the support of these kids and dads was unbelievable. A huge wall-sized card was signed by everyone who attended and tee shirts with the logo "Crew for Drew" were sold. Most moving to us was that Drew's cousin Connor (who also played in the benefit concert) came and had his hair cut off in support. Connor had not cut his hair in six years since losing his father, Drew's Uncle Paul. It was an incredible display of grace and a tribute for a little cousin and we were honored that he chose that event and we know that his dad was very proud of him that day.

Cousin Connor D'Auteuil showing support for his little cousin.

Chapter 11

(written by Pete)
Sunday, December 6, 2009 2:36 PM, EST

Super Sunday! *Hi everyone. I'm sending out this update for all our media-phobia friends (like myself) who have yet to embrace Facebook like Jen and the rest of the world.*

As Jen has alluded to earlier in the week, Drew's ANC (absolute neutrophil count or white blood cells) have been growing exponentially. This morning Drew and I woke up to the exciting news that his ANC count is now 590. That may seem like an arbitrary number, but it's a benchmark for Drew. If Drew is able to sustain an ANC count above 500 for three consecutive days, the medical staff will consider him fully en-grafted. It is one (the most important) of the three benchmarks that would allow Drew to be discharged from the hospital. At this point we are hopeful that if all goes well, Drew will be released to go home next week!

We are not packing our bags just yet because as always, Drew's medical team takes a cautious & conservative approach. The good news that Drew's bone marrow is starting to graft is tempered by the increase risk of Graft vs. Host Disease (GVH). Simply stated, now that Drew has white cells to fight off foreign bodies, there is a higher probability that his body will reject the new bone marrow. The next few weeks should be interesting.

Today Drew and I are back on isolation. Unfortunately one of the patients here on the transplant wing has come down with a respiratory virus. We have to postpone the walks outside his room for the time being until he is cleared. Until then, we are in lock down. It wouldn't be so bad, but unfortunately Drew has decided he rather watch i-Carly than the Patriots vs. Dolphins game! This is cruel and unusual punishment, but I've been bribing him with pizza Bagel Bites so hopefully he will soften his stance and I will catch at least some of the game. Wish me luck.

Until then, keep Drew and our family in your prayers. As you can tell, they are really paying off.

Keep the Faith,
Team D'Auteuil

Even though I was the one who was initially reluctant to have the website for Drew, it had become a sort of therapy for me. From time to time though, Pete would exercise his own writing chops and he updated on one of his days in the unit with Drew. We were still playing the waiting game, but Drew had remained stable and was feeling better every day. We were very relieved that he never developed the horrible mouth sores that usually accompanied transplant patients and thus he didn't need any pain medicine. It was a huge bonus for him. Hope could be overwhelming and we'd feel ourselves starting to get excited and then beat that feeling back down... disappointment was frequent with this illness and we had learned the hard way to try and temper our excitement and remain cautious. "Cautiously optimistic" is a phrase I have come to live with and despise at the same time. We knew that this time would be spent waiting and it could feel never ending. We said "hello" to other parents in the small family kitchen that was there for us, but never really developed any real friendships. It would be too hard to socialize on the unit due to the isolation.

Me and Amy

There was one mom on the same floor that I would run into on occasion and we developed the fast and furious friendship of two moms on the same mission - getting our sick kids out of the hospital. Amy was her name, and her daughter Emily was an oncology patient at Children's. We would meet by chance in the hallway or even in line at the Bertucci's across the street, talk, cry, bitch and moan, hug and be on our way back to our respective rooms. I didn't connect with another mom in the hospital the way I did with Amy. I looked forward to our impromptu meetings in the hallways. Her daughter was facing a different battle, but our journeys were similar and as moms, our feelings were very compatible.

It was December and by now, I should have had the house decorated and we probably would be putting our tree up. Alas, no live plants allowed so there would be no authentic tree in the D'Auteuil household. It was OK. I didn't feel much like celebrating yet and since I had never developed my usual sense of familiar comfort with the changing of the seasons from summer to fall, I certainly hadn't developed any holiday spirit yet. My friend Kendra came over to the house one evening and took the twins to pick out an artificial tree for them to have in the house. It was gestures like these that kept confirming our faith in our friends and family and reminded us to try and focus on getting Drew back to good health. The isolation rooms were essentially our "cells" and we were not inclined to leave Drew for anything longer than to go get dinner or talk to the nurses. We never made use of the gym provided for parents because we didn't like to leave him alone. We relied on our cell phones and email to stay in touch. Seeing him smile every day, watch cartoons and movies, laugh at the clowns, and play games helped keep us focused.

Chapter 12

Tuesday, December 8, 2009 10:26 AM, EST

QUICK UPDATE: *Good morning everyone. Quick update with the latest. Drew's ANC is now 1570! It's actually back in a normal range and we are elated! He now meets that criterion in order to be discharged. The other good news is that yesterday Drew decided to attempt and master the art of swallowing pills. Since he was doing so well, the doctors were transitioning his medications from IV to oral and the multiple liquid meds were not very appealing. Drew is very proud of that accomplishment as are we. We are also closely monitoring daily the new hair growth. He still looks like he's going to be a blond for a while, but Drew and I believe the red will prevail.*

Our only potential setback is that Drew developed a dry cough. He has no fever or other ill symptoms but we can't be too careful and are waiting for the doctors to round to give us some direction. We're hoping that it won't delay his potential discharge this week, but would rather be safe than sorry. Even with his normal ANC, he's still severely immunocompromised and viruses can be very dangerous. Just listening to him cough reminds us how fragile he really is. There was a patient on this unit who tested positive for RSV, a particularly dangerous virus for kids in this unit, but Drew's tests came back negative, thankfully. Unfortunately for us, infection control placed the unit in lockdown for another six days, which means we are limited to this room only. Talk about wanting to climb the walls!

Thanks for checking in with us and celebrating our good news. Please pray that this cough is self limiting and resolves quickly. Please keep our new friends Ethan, Noah, Hannah in your prayers for recovery and continued recovery for Adam and Caroline.

Gratefully,
Team D'Auteuil

We were so close. Damn cough.

Chapter 13

Friday, December 11, 2009 7:14 AM, EST
Homeward Bound....

Enough said.

Chapter 14

Monday, December 14, 2009 3:55 PM, EST

CELEBRATE ME HOME: Hi everyone! We are happy to report that we had a wonderful quiet weekend at home and reported to our first outpatient visit as a post-transplant patient at the Jimmy Fund in Boston this morning. We are also very happy to report more good news that Drew's counts have all skyrocketed and there was no need for any intervention or transfusions today! For all my medical-savvy friends, Drew's ANC was 3580, WBC's 4.87, hemoglobin & hematocrit 10.7/31.8 and platelets rocked the house at 194,000! We are officially "normal!" I can't tell you what a relief it is to cross off "bleeding" from the list of things to be nervous about. Drew's cough still lingers but remains a watch and see. After four months going to the CAT/CR at Children's, we have to get into the routine of going to the Jimmy Fund Clinic and learning all the ins/outs of parking, etc. Fortunately for us, it's right across the street from Children's.

Drew had a special visit from Santa while we were there and two of his elves (check out our new photos). His own personal doctors, Alli O'Neill and Christy Duncan were Santa's helpers today! Drew got a good laugh out of the whole episode and we are so impressed at the lengths his doctors will go to brighten a child's day. Truth be told, they looked like they were having a lot of fun doing it. Alli O'Neill, a second year fellow in hematology and oncology, whom we have mentioned frequently through our website, is still Drew's primary doctor along with Dr. Christy Duncan, who is the director of outpatient transplant care at the Jimmy Fund. We also like her very much and were so happy to see them both today (no matter what they were dressed like!) We also included a photo of Drew's day of discharge from the transplant unit last Friday and the bubble parade that the staff gave them. We loved it, but Drew couldn't care less as he just headed right for the door!

We still have about eight weeks left until we reach that magic 100-day mark and are praying that Drew stays healthy throughout that time. Some of Drew's restrictions lightened up, such as food, but his contact with others is very restricted. We even have *permission to hijack elevators in the clinic for our own personal use. Today, it didn't really matter as the Dana Farber Cancer Institute (which houses the Jimmy Fund) is so ridiculously busy that we couldn't get near an elevator and just took the stairs instead. We are hopeful that as spring starts to approach and we can once again open windows, some of our contact restrictions will be revised. In the meantime, once he feels up to it, we plan on taking Drew skiing with us and he will be allowed to play outside with friends. Drew's doctors continue to tell us how impressive his blood counts are. (Many of the transplant kids still need to be transfused up to a couple of months post transplant. Drew hasn't needed it at all!) Apparently, he received the marrow of Superman. Most likely an Irish Superman, but that's just my opinion.*

In the meantime, to Drew's friends who have been so good about trying to talk on Skype (that means you, Will!), thank you for your perseverance. Drew is coming around. He's still trying to get comfortable with his new look and is encouraged by the hair that is coming in. We're hoping to get him back on Skype soon. We are also pleased to hear that Drew's doctors will allow the best tutor ever to return next month to continue Drew's school work! Yeah Amanda! Drew's looking forward to it!

In closing, thank you again for all your prayers and support and any prayers to spare to our new friends Noah, Ethan, Hannah and Matthew along with Adam and Caroline. I truly believe that your prayers, along with the exceptional staff of Boston Children's and now the Jimmy Fund are responsible for our success so far. I pray that continues.

In gratitude,
Team D'Auteuil

Santa, Drew, Dr. Alli and Dr. Duncan

We were home!! It was a bizarre mix of joy, fear, anticipation and gratitude that we felt, but we were home! Home was isolation, but it was home. No friends or family over for Christmas, but we had our beautiful artificial tree and we were together. It was the best gift. Drew was admitted on November 12th and discharged on December 11th. The team called him a "Rock Star." It was easy to see Drew was happy to be home, too. He was sleeping in his own bed, curling up in his favorite place by the fire to read, and of course, seeing his beloved Ginger lying at his feet. Drew was still in a very fragile state, very weak and easily fatigued, but had come such a long way. I was beginning to allow myself to believe that he was doing it…he was going to beat this, recover and go on to be a normal kid again. I had let my guard down so many times before and regretted it. I was beginning to feel like it was time to let it down again. I continued my regular habit of praying and thanking God every time my mind wasn't occupied with something else.

I nervously hovered around Drew, looking for any sign of anything that would indicate something was wrong. That wasn't new…I started that long before when he first was diagnosed. I still couldn't sleep more than one or two hours at a time and went back to cleaning obsessively through the day and night. I hounded the twins relentlessly about washing their hands and drove them crazy following them around with the hand sanitizer. I could hear a sneeze or sniffle two floors up and would come running to spray it into their hands and followed them around, wiping off every surface they touched. I was trying to get back in tune with their lives as well, contacting their academic team to hear how they were doing and trying to talk to them about what was new in their lives. They had been neglected as a result of circumstance for so long and that only compounded my guilt and anxiety.

I kept up my email correspondence to Jen Barrios and Alaina Palomino, and as a result, our email support network of AA moms was growing slowly. We had now "met" Debbie Erikson and Patty Sprain, two more moms of young AA survivors. I eagerly looked forward to our nearly daily ritual of emailing. Just "talking" to these ladies was so comforting, knowing that we all knew each other's pain. We applauded each other's successes, no matter how small. We supported each other during the painful times, which were many. I was so grateful to have these ladies in my life, despite the circumstances that brought us together.

Chapter 15

Tuesday, December 22, 2009 9:46 AM, EST

HOME FOR THE HOLIDAYS...Part II...?: *Good morning everyone! So far, so good still. Back to Jimmy Fund yesterday for another recheck. Drew's cough and congestion seemed to kick up slightly over the weekend and (this was something new) his white blood cell count was actually a little high. That's unusual for us lately. The doctors felt that it was likely a response to the cold symptoms/sinus congestion that lingers or it was still just his super marrow continuing to acclimate to its new environment. Just to be sure, chest x-rays were clear and sinus films were essentially unchanged. So, they switched one of his antibiotics and will continue to monitor. They still felt that it was a positive sign...one, that his white blood cells were responding and/or two, they were showing that they were capable of responding. His white blood cells have to be educated now to respond to illness and hopefully that's what's happening. Once again, we were showered with praises of how well Drew is doing and we love to hear that.*

Drew continues to feel pretty good, still not a ton of energy but I hope to get him out around the block again today for a little exercise. It's hard when it's so cold out, but enticing him with some hot cocoa upon return seems to help motivate him.

Not much else to report. We return on Thursday to see Alli and hope that we get another positive report. That will be Christmas Eve and we will all be going to the Jimmy Fund as a family that day. We can't do many of our traditional Christmas activities due to our isolation, but we're going to try and at least make a day of it. Wait until the twins find out they have to wake up early....

Yesterday, we received a letter in the mail from the Search Team at Dana Farber asking us if we would like to contact Drew's marrow donor. Are they kidding? We want to have him canonized! However, seeing that's probably not likely, contacting him seems like a comparable consolation prize. We can contact him through the Donor Center anonymously for the first two years. Then after that time period, if he agrees, we can exchange contact information. Pete and I would like to buy him first class airfare and put him up at the Plaza when that time comes. In the meantime, we plan on getting a letter out to him as soon as possible! This young man needs to know how much he has touched our lives. The letters are screened and cannot have any identifying or demographic information. Interestingly, the example they gave of what we cannot write was "our favorite baseball team won the world series twice in four seasons after an 86 year hiatus." I guess they think that might be a little obvious to what area we're from. They are that protective during the first two years. The letter also goes on to say that it is not unusual for donors to decline contact and we are not to take that personally if that's the case, as there are many reasons for that. As long as we are able to fully express how much this young man has touched our lives and know that he received the letter, we'll be okay with that. Anything else would be icing on the cake.

Thanks for checking in with us. Hope to post more positive news and holiday greetings in a few days. Please pray that Drew remains healthy! Thank you!

In appreciation,
Team D'Auteuil

Well, we returned to the Jimmy Fund on Thursday, December 24th to find out that Drew's white blood cell count (WBC) had risen even higher, even though he still felt ok other than a stuffy nose. I could tell Alli was having a difficult time telling us outright, so when I asked if that meant an admission, she simply nodded. Immediately and without restraint, my own tears started falling. Drew saw and asked what was wrong. When I told him he had to be admitted, we were both bawling. It was Christmas Eve. We had brought the twins with us, thinking we'd get some "safe" drive thru fast food and drive around Boston Commons looking at the lights. Instead, I was calling Pete, who had taken the twins down to the local Guitar Center while we waited for labs, and telling him through my sobs that no, I wasn't kidding, he did need to go home and get my overnight bag. It was the first time I didn't bring it and I wanted to kick myself unconscious. Here Drew was, two weeks out of the hospital, home in time for the holidays and he was getting admitted on Christmas Eve. What a slap in the face.

Now, as much as I was hurt for Drew, I was angry. Instead of crying, I wanted to scream every four-letter word I could think of and maybe make up a few new ones. Drew's crying resolved relatively quickly. It wasn't anyone's fault. I can't fault the doctors for taking superior care of Drew. If they felt he should be admitted, then so be it. I would never question their decisions. It didn't mean I had to be happy about it and I wasn't. Pete drove the boys home and then drove back again with my overnight bag. Drew would be getting a CAT scan of his sinuses and would be seen by ENT (ear, nose and throat doctor) that evening. Pete and I quickly formulated a plan for him to drive home (again!) to be with the boys on Christmas Eve and then drive them back to us in the morning to celebrate as best we could in an isolation room in the hospital.

Drew was such a good sport, much better than me. The ENT doctor came to see him and used a tiny telescope, if you will, to take a look up inside Drew's nose. Not the most pleasant of procedures, but he was great with Drew. Very patient and gentle, and it didn't seem to bother him in the least that he was there on Christmas Eve. If it's one thing I learned of all the doctors we had met at Children's, it was they did this because they *wanted* to. You had to be a special person to want to care for children as your chosen life's role. The ENT doctor was pleased that everything actually looked OK. The CAT scan showed just a basic sinusitis. He was started on antibiotics and we settled in for Christmas Eve at the hospital. Drew and I watched "Christmas Vacation," and even though Drew could laugh, I found little humor in one of our favorite holiday films. As soon as he fell asleep, my tears fell again. I couldn't believe we were in the hospital on Christmas Eve. All the pain and frustration of the last six months washed away the hope that I was starting to feel since we'd been home. I didn't sleep much that night, but I was quite used to that by now. Santa stopped by sometime during the night and left Drew a new Nerf machine gun. When he woke up, he couldn't wait to try it out, which wasn't so great for any nurse entering the room. I had him try aiming for the ceiling tiles instead. It hurt so much to see him, actually feeling OK and stuck in this isolation room on Christmas Day. Still, he smiled.

Fortunately, the doctors rounded early and it was shortly after Pete had left home with the twins to visit us at the hospital, that they told me that Drew would be discharged that day. Instead of calling Pete to give him the good news, we decided to wait and surprise him, Kevin and Ryan when they arrived. Needless to say, all three were surprised and elated. Homeward bound again…. We didn't arrive home until about 5:30 PM. No Christmas dinner waiting for us. In fact, no dinner ready at all and Pete and I hadn't wrapped any of the presents we had managed to frantically pick up in the last two weeks when we were home. It was a mad dash in our bedroom haphazardly wrapping while the boys waited impatiently downstairs. The presents weren't wrapped well, the stockings weren't filled and the boys were eating ramen noodles and scrambled eggs for dinner, but it was Christmas and we were home again. Together.

Chapter 16

DAY 57, Let it snow!: *Good evening everyone. Just saw that we're expecting some snow tomorrow night. Another week has gone by and we're still doing great. Drew and I returned to Jimmy Fund yesterday with normal blood counts and more med reductions. I know I talked last week about what a wonderful change it is post-transplant from the multiple weekly visits pre-transplant that we endured and I'm still in awe at the difference. Still, I remain cautiously optimistic each week that passes. One day at a time.*

We almost had a "scare" on Thursday. Alli gave me permission to leave Drew with one or both his older brothers for short trips outside of the house. The boys are well versed on infection control and I always let our neighbors know and have my cell phone on me. I took Kevin to a long-overdue orthodontic appointment and on our way home, Ryan called to say that Drew had slipped and fallen down the stairs. In one instant, my heart fell to the floor. Ryan told me Drew was okay but upset, and after I spoke to Drew and reassured myself that he was okay, I told Ryan that I was almost home. I then started to laugh. Kevin thought I was losing it. Why would I laugh that his little brother had fallen down the stairs?? However, what I was doing was rejoicing! That was the worry that we had for five months...that Drew would slip and fall when his platelets were so critically low and it would be an emergency. It took that little misstep to remind me that there was another thing to be grateful for. To think only now that during those five months, we didn't have any falls. I tried to explain this to Kevin but he still looked at me like I was crazy. That's okay. Aside from a sore butt and ego, Drew was just fine. Just to be certain, he did tell Alli about it yesterday. Alli and I then whoo-hoo'd the fall, the celebration of normal platelets, and then Drew thought I was crazy. All in a day's work.

That's really all for now. I hope to continue boring all of you over the next several weeks. Drew has started to wean off some of his meds and we hope to be extending our time away from the Jimmy Fund over the next two weeks once he's off some of the meds. In the meantime, we've gotten some fresh air dropping the twins off to go skiing and Drew has been able to say hello to Mrs. Ford and Mrs. Boudreau. It's nice to get out a little bit and see some friendly faces. He's still very sensitive to the cold, but that's okay for now. Amanda, the world's best tutor, has returned to Fort Knox and that's helping Drew get back into a schedule during the day and giving him some much needed brain activity. He loves to sit in his favorite chair by the woodstove and read, and has managed to convince Amanda to move the "school room" to that location as well.

I hope you're all enjoying the winter months and got out over the last couple days with the milder weather. Enjoy your Monday holiday and have a wonderful week. Thank you as always for checking in with us.

Keep warm,
Team D'Auteuil

We continued our existence in isolation. Despite all my time worrying about Drew and taking care of him, my loneliness was tough to ignore. Talking on the phone was hard sometimes because it just felt physically exhausting and made me feel distracted. Going out to see friends was simply out of the question. I would not leave Drew unless I absolutely had to. Pete had been slowly getting back on the flight schedule. His co workers, in the ultimate show of support for him, had actually covered his trips for several months now so that I wouldn't be alone caring for Drew. Despite the devastation of this illness, we were still conscious of how incredibly lucky and blessed we were in so many ways.

Drew in his favorite spot by woodstove.

Chapter 17

Sunday, January 31, 2010 9:42 PM, EST

CRUISING, Day 73: *Another week closer to the 100-day mark. Drew saw Alli last Friday with another great exam and blood counts. In the next two weeks, he will wean off several more medications, and hopefully his central line will come out about that time as well. All positive things to look forward to. Still, we rejoice carefully, taking each day one at a time.*

We continue to try and get Drew to be a little more active and social and we have noticed that he's asking us to go out in the car a little bit more. He enjoys the rides to Crotched Mountain to drop off his brothers to ski, or to say hello to their friends if we drop the twins off somewhere else. I think seeing the twins' friends and their families is helping elevate his confidence and comfort with his appearance. He continues to struggle with the cold intolerance. However, today when he asked to

get out of the house, we made a plan to go see Aunt Dayna's horses and when we got there, Uncle John had fired up the tractor. As you can see by the picture, Drew was in heaven. I haven't seen him light up like that in months. Even after spending time driving the tractor, stopping to see the horses at Chappell farm and then feeding Aunty Dayna's horses and dog Sophie, Drew was not complaining about the cold. It's the longest he's been out in months. Definitely an uplifting day.

Thanks for continuing to check up on us. Every week, there is something that happens to remind me of how much people are thinking of Drew and it's just an amazing feeling. Just this week, Coach Dodge dropped off a signed framed print of a "Champion" poem signed by the champs of our own Amherst Patriots. It's now proudly displayed next to the coveted helmet of the Souhegan-Merrimack Turkey Bowl, which the team signed as well. Ever-present reminders of how blessed we are to live in such an amazing town.

I hope that you are staying warm. Those hardy New England boys still ski despite the single-digit readings on the thermometer and one must be impressed with their devotion to their sport. Time to say good night and wish you all a wonderful week.

Team D'Auteuil

I tried to keep up the feel of "normal" in my house as much as possible. Drew fortunately, was quite content to keep a low profile and enjoy the heat of the woodstove while he read or did his homework. Amanda still made school fun for him and both of us looked forward to her arrival every afternoon to break up the monotony of our days. I was still cooking according to the immunocompromised restrictions and wasn't having much luck making anything very interesting. Drew's appetite was still a bit off and he was still vomiting frequently due to his medications. We all longed for salads and fresh fruit. It didn't feel right to eat that in front of Drew, so we all went without. I scoured grocery stores searching for the permitted frozen berries that weren't imported. It was turning into a long winter, but every day we were home was a good day.

While I continued running the house in keeping with our guidelines of immunocompromised living, it didn't take much to make me panic or second-guess a decision I made, past or present. For example, my good friend Kathy Ford called me one day while I was systematically removing all my plastic containers from my cabinets and into trash bags. I had heard about BPA (bisphenol A) on the news - a plastic product used in containers and some canned foods. There were safety concerns about this chemical leaching into food from BPA-treated plastic containers and cans, and the risks from this were not well-defined yet. I did some research and discovered that there were numbers printed on the bottles/containers that would tell you if that particular container was safe or not. In keeping with my mentality at the time, they were all deemed toxic and thus, they had to go. As I was telling Kathy this, and also worrying that she would think I'd really lost my mind this time, she commented that she had also heard something about that and started going through her plastic containers while we spoke. Good friends never let you go crazy alone.

Chapter 18

Friday, February 5, 2010 2:32 PM, EST

DON'T STOP BELIEVING, DAY 78: *Good afternoon everyone! What a gorgeous day! I'm really hoping for a busy, but great weekend ending with a family Super Bowl Sunday celebration. Yes, it would be better if another team was playing, but we won't go down that road.*

    Check out Drew and Amanda dissecting squids this afternoon! So cool!!!

*   We return from yet another great visit at Jimmy Fund. Once more, Drew's counts were absolutely normal and we are just ecstatic! He only has one week left of steroids and his doctors are so pleased with his progress. We are too! We have*

seen a return of Drew's upbeat personality including requests to go see friends after school and there's a rumor circulating that he may even venture down to the school at recess to say hello one of these days! Alli also confirmed what I saw the other night and that is...hair!! It's not much, but there's definitely a sign of growth! Drew doesn't fully appreciate it yet since it's hard for him to see, but it's definitely there!

After reviewing Drew's counts and checking him over head to toe, Alli and the attending doctor reviewed the plan again from here. Drew will wean off steroids next week and with that, he will also stop a couple of other meds that will no longer be needed. Shortly after that, he will begin the slow wean of his cyclosporine, which is the immunosuppressant that inhibits rejection of his new marrow. That will take about six months to complete. At that time, he'll be about nine months post transplant. That leaves then three months still of strict indoor contact/avoidance isolation. You would think that the gradual weaning of the meds and the time passage would enable Drew re-enter the "world" so to speak, but alas, that's not the case. Children's philosophy of strict isolation is backed up by their studies, and the way they explained it to me today was that once his body has fully accepted and adjusted to his new marrow (which was under the influence of immunosuppressants that kept it from being rejected), it would be "cruel" to force it into the world without first operating on its own for a while. Unfortunately, it means Drew will not be able to attend school for a while next fall but we're more than willing to abide by their recommendations to see this through.

I don't know if Drew caught on yet that he wouldn't be able to start school next year, but the doctors did address that there was a possibility of maybe some gradual progression toward the classroom this coming fall. We won't think about it yet. We'll just plan on more tutoring until we reach that 365 day mark and get the OK. It's best to be thinking practically.

So it's time to start planning the Super Bowl Feast! We can't buy our usual football cake from Market Basket so Drew has asked me to bake a football cake. Alli had a better idea for me and told me to make a sheet cake and just decorate it as a field. Much more my speed! Not sure how I would have made a football...?

Have a great weekend everyone!
Team D'Auteuil

Time definitely felt like it was moving very slowly in the house. Our routine was monotonous, but we were home and each day was a day closer to fewer medications and recovery. Amanda did her best to keep Drew entertained with school and we both continued to look forward to her arrival every day. She was the only one that the doctors allowed in our house. They were so strict, but they valued education and we were very grateful to have that link to the outside world. Kevin and Ryan were plugging away at school, but I know they were very distracted and worried. It was difficult for them to focus all the time. It was also hard on them not being allowed to have anyone in the house. They had a number of loyal friends who would come over despite not being allowed inside, and hang out in the screened porch. During the winter months, the boys built a ski rail in the backyard and their friends would come over to use that. They would huddle in the screen porch and I would bring them hot cocoa or apple crisp. It was shortly after several of these afternoon visits that I noticed all the yellow spots on the snow. I thought Ginger must have been peeing in the backyard which was unusual because she was "woods trained." Then it hit me…all those boys… not allowed in the house to use the bathroom. Oh, well. I was just grateful that they were such good friends to the twins.

Chapter 19

Saturday, February 13, 2010 4:41 PM, EST

THE NUMBERS GAME, DAY 86: *Good afternoon faithful members of Drew's Army! We hope you all have a wonderful weekend. Valentine's Day tomorrow and the kids have no school on Monday! I know there's lots of skiing going on.*

    Another successful visit to Jimmy Fund on Friday. Drew's counts remain totally normal and three meds were discontinued yesterday and another one finishes up on Monday. That is huge! The talks are in place to get his line out sometime in the next week or so. That subject is a little touchy for Drew, as he's so accustomed to his line and hasn't needed to be stuck in over three months. The thought of getting it out actually was less appealing than we thought it would be. We're spending the next week intermittently discussing with him how great it will be to be free of it: the daily care, the wrapping/taping to shower, etc. The biggest advantage is that once it is removed, our visits will transition to once every 2-3 weeks!

    Several months ago, a friend of mine advised me to try not to play the "numbers game." Focusing on statistics, outcomes and studies would just drive me insane. I may not be clinically insane yet, but I've been very open about the OCD I seem to have developed to help deal with the loss of control this whole ordeal has caused. As much as I tried to avoid focusing on the numbers, it seemed every time I turned around there was another "number" jumping out at me. Watching Drew's counts for example. All his counts are numbered. We learned quickly the ranges for each and every blood count Drew had. Every aspect of Drew's treatment involved numbers: what his counts were, how many units of blood he would need, how many minutes it would take, how many days in between infusions, how many weeks until first chemo would be considered a failure, how many hours a day for second chemo, how many radiation treatments, measuring what went in and what came out, numbers, numbers, numbers!

Taking his temperature used numbers. All his medications are dosed by numbers. We couldn't leave the hospital until his ANC was over 500 for three days. More numbers. I can't get away from it! After a while it becomes part of your life. In that same moment, you realize how much numbers are a part of your life anyway. We're surrounded by numbers. The time. Channels on the TV and radio stations are numbers. Your address is full of numbers. There's no American Airlines Flight ABC. You get a number at the deli. You put 16 gallons of gas in your car. It's all numbers!

Now, for us, the next number is in two short weeks. Day 100. Another milestone that was difficult for us to even imagine back on November 18th (another number), yet it's just around the corner. I will thank my friend for giving me that advice, for it wasn't totally in vain. I just had to learn to play the numbers game one day at a time. Maybe someday I'll write a book called "The 12 Steps of the Other AA." Maybe. I'll probably need a lot of therapy first.

In closing, Drew has had a fantastic week! He's made it outside several days to see some friends for the first time in months. To see his smile and old personality returning is such an incredible thing to witness. He also was able to see his hair that's coming in now! Hopefully, it will hurry up. Mr. Lambrou has let us know that once warm weather returns, he holds a fifth grade gym class outside every day and invited Drew to join! Drew is very psyched. Pete and I will try and get him to Crotched next week to possibly try maybe just one skiing run. Getting him outside with friends is awesome, as we can now see how deconditioned he is after so many months of decreased activity and then just his transplant. We can't wait for warmer weather! Spring is in 35 days!! (Couldn't resist adding that number!)

Happy Valentine's Day!
Team D'Auteuil

That magic 100-day milestone we had been intently focused on was coming soon! I had been cultivating this daydream where the 100th day meant that life would be smooth sailing from there on in. I set myself up for that daydream and actually started to believe it, despite my sleepless nights and chronic anxiety. Drew seemed to be working his way through recovery so smoothly. I was allowed to daydream, wasn't I? It just had to happen that way. Drew had been through so much. He deserved it!

Chapter 20

Sunday, February 21, 2010 4:26 PM, EST

MILESTONES AND FALSE ALARMS: *Good afternoon and thank you to everyone who prayed for Drew. Prayers were answered and we are back home after a long morning that capped off a long week. Where to begin? I'll try and condense it, for so much has happened this past week and most of it was positive!*

First, Drew completed reading Harry Potter 6 & 7 in six days! We thought that was pretty impressive and worth mentioning.

Second, Drew had "old faithful," his central line, removed last Wednesday after five days of discussion with both Drew and his doctor. Together they made the decision that the time was right. This was a big milestone and a grownup decision for Drew to take part in. After all, after 3 1/2 months, it had become part of him and to remove it created some anxiety about getting stuck again. Too bad the timing actually stunk, as no one could have predicted the turn of events that waited for him, but more about that later.

Third, as you can tell by the picture, Drew made it skiing with me last Thursday! Drew has been skiing since he was four but after very little physical activity for nine months and subsequent BMT, he's really not very conditioned. That will take some time. However, he made it down the bunny slope twice to warm up and then down SuperNova once before he was too tired to continue. His form and skill were still evident. I was so proud of him!

Thursday night, Drew woke with

right upper abdominal pain and vomiting that lasted about 1 hour then it went away. I talked to the doctor on call and it was decided that since Drew didn't have a fever we would wait and see Alli as planned the next morning. Friday morning, we arrived in Boston and we could tell Drew wasn't quite feeling himself but denied any pain. He did vomit again but we felt that was probably the anxiety surrounding getting stuck four times for a blood draw, (remember I told you the timing of the line removal wasn't so great??) After the first labs were back, we were discharged early since Drew had been so rock stable for 92 days. However, Murphy's Law is Murphy's Law and that's literally my name. We weren't home very long before we got the call that Drew's liver tests were elevated. I could get into a lengthy dissertation of everything going on, but suffice it to say, we needed to return to Boston for more tests and an ultrasound. The big worry was infection or rejection. We were so lucky that Frannie, Drew's favorite nurse from the CAT/CR stayed late for Drew to draw his blood and of course, got it in one try! We were so grateful to her!! Thank you Frannie!! We left that night nervous but thankful the ultrasound was normal, but there was a gallstone that even I noticed. We talked to Alli and it was agreed for us to return Tuesday for repeat labs.

Then last night, Alli called to say that Drew's liver tests had skyrocketed and in only a few hours, I noticed the whites of his eyes had yellowed slightly. After several phone calls and much discussion with the team, they decided to have us return this morning and admit him for probable graft vs. host disease (GVHD) with liver involvement. I haven't felt that scared in a couple months. Drew's recovery has been so miraculous that we were spoiled, and the thought of this scared us silly. We tried our best to keep that from Drew and help his anxiety about getting stuck again.

We arrived this morning, packed for staying and went to the ER as planned for labs and to see the team. I know that I've mentioned before that I've never been one to evangelize, but I'm also not afraid to admit my faith. Last night I asked for prayers and despite the simplicity of what is assumed happened to Drew Thursday night to explain his symptoms and lab results, I believe in my heart that it was prayer that played the biggest role. I will never underestimate its power and I'm thankful every day for my faith and the faith of my friends and family who have prayed for us throughout this ordeal. For that's what it is, an ordeal. Yes, there is always something good that comes out of something bad. There are always life lessons and events to make you reflective and grateful, but it's still an ordeal and there are times it's very hard. So, thank you everyone who prayed. From the bottom of my heart, thank you.

So, here's the kicker. It was likely the gallstone that created the mess that is *the last 36 hours - Drew's symptoms Thursday night, the sudden skyrocketing of liver tests and subsequent plummeting of the labs back to almost normal. Graft vs. host really wouldn't do that in such a manner. So, what does that mean for us? Not much. We watch and see. I will continue to thank God every day that it wasn't GVHD and hope that Drew doesn't have another symptomatic episode. Drew is unusually young for gallstones, but given his restricted diet, medications and BMT, any one of those or a combination could have contributed to this. In any case, once again, NO GVHD!!!*

So, that's all I have tonight. Exhaustion and gratitude. Thank you Geni and Missy H for taking my calls and continuing to take such great care of my boys and I know how much each of you probably loves two extra teens in your house! Thank you so much! Thank you to everyone for prayers and support. This was a scary weekend for us and we made it through with your help. I hope everyone has a great vacation week!

Just one more:

"I prayed to the LORD and he answered me, freeing me from all my fears." **Psalm 34:4-18 (NLT)**

Gratefully,
Team D'Auteuil

The gallbladder. For Drew, this small organ, located just to the right of the stomach, had become quite an annoyance. The gallbladder, which mainly aids in fat digestion, decided to rebel after the assault from Drew's treatment and many meds. The doctors reassured us that this is a very common complication of BMT. Their primary goal was to coax it along until a time when it was safe to remove, if necessary. That meant some dietary management. Not easy when you can't eat anything fresh and most of the safe foods were deep fried, but we did our best. Good thing Drew loved his Cheerios. Hopefully, this was just a one-time occurrence.

Chapter 21

Saturday, February 27, 2010 2:36 PM, EST

100 DAYS!!! My rainbow is overdue: *Good afternoon everyone! 100 days... unbelievable to think that it's been that long already. Almost 1/3rd of the way through recovery. Back on November 18th, it wasn't even possible to stretch our minds to this date, but here we are! You'll have to excuse my not-so-subtle borrowing of a cheesy line from an old, but favorite, Bad Company song as my lead in this week. I heard it on the radio the other day and it seemed an appropriate thought for us at this time. I also heard another song recently by Miley Montana, or whatever her name is, but since Drew isn't her biggest fan, decided to go with the oldie. After last week, this week has been nicely low-key. We returned to Jimmy Fund yesterday to see Alli and Drew has normal counts once again. So normal, in fact, that we are not scheduled to return for two weeks!*

Many people have asked us what the 100 days mean. In short, the most critical time period of recovery after a bone marrow transplant is the first 100 days. As Alli and Dr. Steve reviewed with us yesterday, although it's a milestone, it's an arbitrary number. The first 100 days was when Drew was most susceptible to infection and acute graft vs. host disease (GVHD). Although that time has passed and Drew's counts look normal on paper, not much will change for us as far as our new style of living. Drew is still highly susceptible to infection and GVHD can always show up when you least expect it. We are still on strict isolation until the next 265 days are over but we're looking forward to a fairly "normal" summer when Drew can be outside. I'm already looking into some SPF clothing, as Drew will have to be really careful about sun exposure, as that can trigger GVHD. As if my fair skinned boy didn't have enough to worry about with the sun.

This is vacation week for most of us and with Kevin and Ryan keeping friends company skiing this week, we've been trying to keep Drew busy. Tuesday he went snow tubing with a few friends at McIntyre. He and Pete had a Harry Potter movie marathon this week and now they are both anxiously awaiting the

69

release of the seventh movie. Aunt Denise, Sully, Sarah and Connor sent Drew personalized M&M's with the words "100 Days and Counting" on them! How cool is that??!! In keeping with the "Drew's Army" theme, they are bright orange. I'm curious to see how long they last.

Lastly, we are in the planning stages of a 100 Days celebration for Drew. I will post something here and on my FB page once it's settled. We're planning an outdoor ice cream sundae drop-in event for all friends and family who would like to stop by and wish Drew congratulations. The date, time and place will be firmed up by early next week. Stay tuned!!

So, that's all for now. The pesky gallstone has not resurfaced and we hope that it decides to remain out of sight (and out of his bile duct). Our weather the last few days has been interesting to say the least and I hope most of you have your power turned back on. Here's hoping for an uneventful two weeks for us and a great two weeks for everyone else! I don't have my calendar in front of me, but I think it's now about three weeks until spring!

Gratefully,
Team D'Auteuil

My excitement and confidence grew as I quickly planned a 100-day celebration for Drew. I knew better now than to plan too far ahead. I decided on a "Sundaes on Sunday" theme and set about the plans. Porter Dodge, the principal at the Amherst Middle School where Drew should have been attending, allowed us to use the parking lot at the school to host this event. I started on my shopping list and was feeling quite confident that this would come together swiftly and easily. Nothing could stop me now!

Chapter 22

Tuesday, March 2, 2010 4:42 PM, EST
%^&*#%@!) GALLBLADDER: My Rainbow is overdue, part II:

Back home again after our unexpected temporary residence at Child-Hilton-ren's in Boston. Drew's very happy to be back home and we took a quick detour to Aunty Dayna's on the way home for a quick outside visit. After successfully reducing most of Drew's meds the last few weeks, they have changed one and added one, and another "just in case" med for nausea. Drew's gallbladder attack nearly three weeks ago seemed to have set off a systemic response of vomiting intermittently but it finally seems to be slowing down and all counts have returned to normal (or near normal for some post transplant counts). Drew was admitted primarily to get some fluids back into him. Vomiting is a cycle which can perpetuate itself and we are now in the process of breaking that cycle. In any event, home is much better. Instead of having our two week break as planned from returning to Jimmy Fund, we will return this Friday to see Alli for a quick check. However, we did hear a rumor that we will then not have to return until another two weeks after that. I'll believe it when it happens. Last time we planned that, we didn't make it two days. Better to be prepared.

That's really about it. Thanks for checking with us. We hope everyone had a great vacation. It feels like spring is in the air today but I heard something about more snow this week. I don't think Kevin and Ryan are quite ready to hang up their skis yet.

Have a great week!
Team D'Auteuil

Drew's vomiting had been a near-daily event for many months. The gallbladder problems just made it worse and more unpredictable. It was during this time that we learned of Ginger's devotion to Drew and a unique talent she possessed that took a little time to figure out. When we'd hear

Drew get sick (he never seemed to have any warning and couldn't call to us in time), we would find Ginger with him. Since Drew spent most of his time in our finished basement TV/playroom, the only place in the house Ginger wasn't allowed, we would scold her to leave and she'd sulk off sadly while we attended to Drew. In truth, we were worried that she wanted to eat the vomit or some other disgusting thing like that. She is a dog, after all. In time, we started to notice Ginger taking off like a shot and observed her without any hesitation running down the stairs to the playroom. *Then* we would hear Drew getting sick. We realized that she somehow could sense right before he got sick! Once we realized it, we felt terrible that we had been scolding her and hugged and praised her, showering her with dog treats. We realized that she only wanted to be by his side when he was sick, or maybe this was her way of protecting him or alerting us that he was sick. We then used Ginger as a "vomit-o-meter" so we knew when Drew was about to get sick. Silly parents, dogs are for kids.

Chapter 23

Sunday, March 7, 2010 6:33 PM, EST

SUNDAES ON SUNDAY RECIPE!:
8 gallons of ice cream
6 cans whipped cream
6 jars of chocolate fudge
2 jars caramel
2 jars chocolate shell
3 bags of gummy bears
2 bags mini m&m's
2 containers of sprinkles
+a whole lot of friends and family

_____

= the best celebration ever!

What an unbelievable day! What a great turnout and what an amazing reminder of how blessed we are! So many friends and family came to wish Drew congratulations for this wonderful milestone. Drew's sweatshirt with "100 Days" on it was courtesy of Aunty Dayna and Uncle John. Thank you!! The warm weather, brilliant sunshine and bright blue sky seemed to have been made to order for this special occasion. It was so great to see everyone, friends and family, who came from near and far. Thank you so much for sharing this day with us! To everyone who helped out with the "hands free" sundae bar (Lori, Leanne, Jen R., Kara, Robin and everyone else) thank you! Thank you to Jay Marciano for taking photos (I can't wait to see them!) and Aunt Dayna and Uncle John for taking the photos for my Facebook page. Thank you to the Fords and Swartzes for the use of your tables. Thank you Steve Nelson for just showing up and reminding us that you are now more than nine years post transplant. You are an inspiration for us! Thank you to Mr. Dodge and the Amherst Middle School for the use of the parking lot. Most of all, thank you everyone for prayers that made this celebration possible. We can never thank you enough.

Drew had such a good time and seeing all his friends was so uplifting for him. He was a little tired, but very happy. To see him that happy is all I needed. He hasn't been around this many people in months! To see him among kids playing on the basketball courts, tennis courts and climbing what's left of the snow banks brought me as close to a feeling of joy that I've felt since he was diagnosed. True joy will come when we hear those magic words that he is cured.

Drew's older brothers Kevin and Ryan turned 15 on March 5th and their birthday celebration was somewhat mingled with this celebration. They have sacrificed a lot in the past nine months and I'm very proud of them for the way they have stood by their little brother. Happy birthday to my boys!

It is now 108 days since Drew's transplant and nine months since that day that our hearts stopped and have since struggled to beat against the weight of fear, pain and the unknown. Today, they beat a little stronger. We are surrounded by one of the best medical teams in the world and the love and support of family and friends who let us know on a daily basis that they have our backs. You will never know how much you carry us. Thank you to God for all of you and all that we have.

Thank you to everyone for making this a wonderful day! We are very grateful to everyone! Right now, I have to go tuck in a very tired, but very happy boy.

All our love,
Team D'Auteuil

We could almost feel true happiness again. We were gifted with the most beautiful day and unseasonably warm weather for this great event. The turnout was huge and I was full of pride at Drew's stamina and for reaching this milestone. While I was assisted by several friends and family members, all donning gloves and dishing out ice cream and toppings in accordance with the immunosuppressant guidelines, I kept an eye on my son as he navigated in and out of the crowd. The turnout, the sunshine and the overall feeling of relief at reaching this milestone, made me believe that Drew was well on his way to beating AA. We were almost one third of the way to that magic one-year mark and we couldn't wait for that celebration! I allowed myself to start thinking about how to celebrate....

Friend and fellow BMT survivor Steve Nelson and Drew

Drew and Will Facques

Chapter 24

"SPRINGBREAK 2010" DAY 121: Happy first day of spring! I have been thinking a lot about seasons lately. I have been so happy to experience this warm weather and be able to be outside, feeling normal. Something we haven't experienced in a long time. It struck me this week that it was spring of last year that this nightmare started. It was just a few weeks before summer. Hard to believe it's been that long, yet harder to believe that it's only been that long. I know I've tried to describe before the suffocating sensation of not being able to move while the world revolves at an alarming pace around you. It's as if you're standing still and witnessing everyday life pass by you. The warm weather this week and being able to get outside and enjoy it has opened a window in which we can reach out and feel what it's like to be back, almost in sync with the rest of the world. It's a positive feeling. I'm in denial about the possible return to more season-appropriate weather of slightly cooler temps, but the last week helped us tremendously.

Well, back to business. We are pleased and proud to announce that we made it two weeks between Jimmy Fund visits! This marks the first time ever that we went that long between visits to Children's. Prior to this, the longest we ever went was one week and we managed to do that three times last September. We thought that was a break. This was awesome and the timing with the beautiful weather couldn't have been better! We are also pleased and proud to announce that once again, Drew's counts are all normal! If you didn't know Drew's history and looked at his labs, you would wonder why he even had them done. It's simply amazing to think about. Alli and the team told us again yesterday how pleased they are with his progress and his wonderful start to his recovery.

The only other issue is a very faint rash that Drew noticed on his hands about two days ago. The doctors decided that it looked like just a little bit of GVHD. Although the initial mention of that acronym sent shivers down my spine, the attending quickly explained that not only do they generally expect this to appear, they almost welcome it as a sign that the marrow knows what it's supposed to do...recognize something as foreign and try to reject it. Since Drew's immunosuppressant levels were great and the rash is so minimal, they were not too concerned. In my mind, I likened it to more of a "picket line" than a actual "strike." Our only job is to monitor it this week and let them know if it gets worse. Drew's gallbladder seems to have settled down nicely and hopefully will not remind us again of its potential to wreak havoc. At least we now know what to expect should that happen again. Otherwise, we will return to Jimmy Fund in another two weeks!!

We have plans in place to get Drew "back in school" via Skype to observe some lessons and also get him to recess and eventually outdoor gym class. Drew still tires easily but the more we get him moving, the more his energy level should gradually return. The last couple of weeks have helped his confidence and desire to reconnect with kids his own age. He's been surrounded by adults for the last six months and could use a healthy dose of fifth grade antics to feel like a normal kid again. It also helps that the hair is coming in at a high-velocity speed. Drew has even shown a few close friends and family members and that's a tremendous sign of growth and confidence. Several of Drew's friends have offered to walk to our house after school to play for an hour or two and that is such an awesome gift to us and Drew really looks forward to it.

It's too beautiful out to spend on the computer. I hope you all get outside to enjoy this beautiful day and the first of spring. It's been a long time coming to us and we need to get outside and welcome it! Pete took the twins to Sunapee today for some spring skiing with friends and Drew and I will be hanging out a little more and plan to get out this afternoon to see some friends. Great plan for a beautiful day!

> **"He fills my life with good things. My youth is renewed like the eagle's!"** Psalm 103:5-15 (NLT)

Happily,
Team D'Auteuil

Waiting and waiting. AA and BMTs are definitely not illnesses or treatment for those with limited patience, such as myself. I was working on it. I wasn't given a choice. I had to work on developing patience. It was a challenge every day to be grateful just for that day. I found myself surrounded with quotes and quips about daily life and challenges, from greeting cards to the books that I occasionally found time to pick up. Things like "God only gives you what you can handle" and stuff like that. I don't buy it. God didn't "give" us this. God didn't give Drew AA. It happened. Do I believe that God *knew* it was going to happen? Yes. But I choose to believe that God knows what you're about to be given and then *helps* you handle it. There's a distinct difference.

Chapter 25

HAPPY EASTER! Day 136: Easter greetings everyone! We hope you are enjoying the beautiful weather this weekend. It's been two weeks since I last updated and I am ecstatic to report that we made it the two weeks again to our scheduled appointment at Jimmy Fund last Friday and had a wonderful visit. Drew's counts were perfect and the doctors told us and Drew again how pleased they are with his recovery so far. The best news is that we now have three weeks off until the next visit! I have to be honest when I say that I was quite conflicted about that news. My first reaction was one of complete happiness and then one of "what?? Three weeks?? What are they thinking making us wait three weeks??" It's the strangest combination of relief and anxiety. However, aside from the possibility of missing Alli after not seeing her for three weeks, Drew was very happy! I'm sure that I'll be fine as well.

This weekend has been wonderful for a number of reasons. Besides the beautiful weather, Drew had a great time biking with buddies and coloring Easter eggs outside yesterday. Today we plan on visiting family and friends this afternoon for quick visits as we celebrate the first holiday spent at home in the last year. It's quite something to realize that Easter of '09 was the last holiday that we celebrated as a family at home. Every holiday since that time we spent at Children's.

Drew has realized this past week that it is tough to get reconditioned after all that he's been through, and this weekend he made an admirable attempt to push himself a little bit physically. He has also accepted defeat with the sunscreen battle and is showing great motivation with applying it himself without being hounded about it. I was able to find quite a bit of sun protective clothing at Bob's and Target and thus he has a new spring/summer wardrobe. The new items will also come in handy for Atlantis in ten months! I made sure to buy it all too big for him. He has also transitioned to the baseball cap for the warmer weather. He also had a confidence surge as his buddy Will was the first to glimpse the "crewcut" that Drew is now sporting. Will's response..."cooool."

We have also been adjusting Drew's daily schedule into one with a little more structure. Drew is now Skyping math, science and DARE three days a week and we'll probably add another day over the next week or so. We'll also probably start attending recess now that the warmer weather has arrived and think about gym class once they're held outside. Drew definitely would benefit from being around more kids his own age instead of just adults. He has missed nearly a year of social development and it's so much better for him to have conversations and activities more suitable to fifth graders than worrying about current world events. (Not that we're opposed to him knowing about world events, but at 11 years old, we would rather he be concerned about more age-appropriate things.) Amherst Middle School continues to be very accommodating and we're very grateful to Mrs. Kim, Mrs. Gagne and Mrs. Nedelman for their assistance. Mrs. Kim has also trained a couple of Drew's friends to work the laptop in her absence. Thank you!

Drew has decided appropriately that the soccer team would likely be too much for him at this point. However, he and Dad plan on watching the games and rooting for "his" team. Kevin and Ryan have started lacrosse and we all plan on attending the games as a family. All these outdoor activities will hopefully help Drew feel reconnected with the rest of the world. The restrictions still in place annoy him at times because it still makes him feel "different" but there's something comforting about the fact that he is protesting them. The spark is reassuring to us that he's intent on beating this. Besides, we have this restriction thing down to a science. There isn't anything we can't work around or offer a suitable substitute. I think I'll write a "how to" book for parents sometime in the future.

The forecast for the rest of the week looks very promising. I'm at home waiting for Pete to come home from church with Kevin and Ryan. The sun is shining and we have a great afternoon planned. We hope you are all enjoying this beautiful day and holiday. We are finding things to be grateful for every day and today is no different. We are home as a family celebrating the most sacred of Christian holy days. We don't find that to be a coincidence.

Happy Easter Everyone!!

"He is not here; he has risen!" Luke 24:6 (NIV)

Feeling positive,
Team D'Auteuil

I dared to allow myself the thought that our life was returning to a semi-normal status, despite our isolation. I was still lonely and still confined myself in the house to take care of Drew, but the thought of eventually stepping out to see friends again or do something other than doctors' appointments or quick trips to the grocery store were beginning to enter my mind with more fervor. I daydreamed about attending lacrosse games with Drew to watch his brothers play and the socializing that accompanies those sporting events. After all, Drew was doing so well!

Saturday, April 10th, Drew spent the afternoon with his friend Zach. It was a beautiful day and they went out biking. Pete then spent some time in the backyard with them playing soccer. Drew, however, sat down on the grass and refused to play saying he was too tired. I'll admit, we were a little disappointed. Things had been going so well and we were trying to push him a little to challenge himself to rebuild his stamina and strength. He wouldn't budge. He had a mild cough for a couple of days, but I had emailed Alli the day before and said that I would watch him and let her know if things got worse. Our friends, Leanne and Howie, had invited us to dinner. Pete and I went over for dessert. We couldn't be out long enough for dinner *and* dessert. It was our first time out since the transplant. The fact that they were just a short drive up the road was also reassuring since we were so close to home. We had a wonderful evening, short as it was, and then went home. It was then that I heard Drew coughing.

I went upstairs and listened to his lungs. He sounded a bit wheezy. He was tired and aggravated with me, but I made him take an Albuterol nebulizer treatment. Drew had reactive airway disease before his transplant, commonly referred to as "childhood asthma." The doctors couldn't say whether or not he'd still have it post transplant. Since Drew's symptoms were always triggered by a cold, it looked like he still had it. During the night, he would be OK for about three hours and then I would have to give him another nebulizer treatment because he would start coughing again. By morning, he looked better and was acting fine, but I called the doctor on-call anyway, thinking I should at least let them know I had started the nebulizer treatments. I had been in touch with Alli during the week and even emailed her on Friday to say that Drew's cough hadn't changed and I didn't think he needed to come in. The on-call doctor thought it best to bring him in. I wasn't convinced and even went so far as to ask if it was really necessary, something I have never done, but she was gentle but firm that it was best to come in and make sure it was nothing else. This was a moment that will come back to me. I felt something. Not my gut, not anxiety. Just *something?* A strange, fleeting sensation that I couldn't really identify or understand. It's nearly impossible to explain and maybe it was the doctor's gentle insistence, but I agreed to bring him in. My gut instinct was not on high alert or even activated. Pete and the boys had plans, so I told him to go ahead with their day and I would bring Drew. I would call him later on. I was certain it was just asthma and we'd be home later on.

In the ER, Drew had a chest x-ray and then the doctors told me it looked like he had pneumonia. I looked over at Drew as he sat on the ER stretcher laughing at a movie. I was shocked. He didn't have a fever and he certainly didn't act sick. He just had this nagging cough that seemed to be increasing just since we arrived. I still wasn't panicked. Once I learned he was going to be admitted (this time I brought my overnight bag, just in case), I called Pete, told him we were fine and I would keep him posted. Drew was scheduled for a CAT scan of his lungs. Still, no panic. I went over to the CVS in the lobby of the hospital and picked up a bag of Doves chocolates, a Gatorade for Drew and a couple of bottles of water since he didn't like what they stocked on the unit. Drew had his CAT scan and vomited as they were getting him off the table. Since he vomited all the time, it didn't phase me much.

Soon after the CAT scan, we were brought to our room on the transplant unit. As I tried to write an update on his website and answer some email, Drew kept calling my attention to a movie he was watching at the time. He wanted me to watch with him. I remember almost getting impatient with him. I was busy and I had probably seen the movie almost as many times as he had! A little while later, I asked him if he wanted anything to eat and he said no. It wasn't until he decided around 9 PM that he was tired and wanted to go to sleep that he looked a little "off" to me and had started to cough a little more frequently. I shut off the movie and gave him a kiss goodnight. Shortly after he fell asleep, the nurse came in to get his vitals. Again, I was almost annoyed. He had just fallen asleep. When she checked his pulse oximeter, the measure of oxygen in your bloodstream, it said 91%. It should be between 97-100% I asked her if that was accurate. Just as I asked that, I noticed that his blood pressure was very low, about 80/40. Now, I was worried.

Over the next two hours, in between the nurses hanging more IV fluids to raise his blood pressure and the respiratory therapists into administer oxygen and nebulizer treatments, the BMT doctor came in to tell me that they were concerned that Drew had pneumocystis pneumonia, a rare pneumonia that immunocompromised patients were susceptible to. His condition was progressing rapidly she told me, and there was a team from the ICU coming down to evaluate him. Drew continued to plead to sleep and between the coughing, the nurses checking him and respiratory therapists, he wasn't getting any. During this time, Alli called me on the room telephone to offer some support. I called Pete and told him I didn't know what was happening, but it was happening fast and to get down here.

The whole time I watched Drew get worse before my eyes, I mentally beat myself up. Where was my gut instinct? Why didn't I see this coming? Why didn't I call during the night before when I needed to give him three nebulizer treatments? My gut instinct, from day one, had been right on the money when it came to knowing how serious his illness was, when he had a fever, when he'd need platelets and most crushing was that I knew in my heart that he'd need a bone marrow transplant. I just kept that inside because I refused to cave to fear and forced myself to hope, but my gut was almost always right. I had let my guard down and become arrogant in his recovery so far. Now, in the transplant unit over the next two hours, the doctors and nurses were unable to keep his blood pressure or oxygen at stable levels so he was going to be transferred to the ICU. It was about 1 AM, he was exhausted, and all he wanted to do was sleep. Pete arrived just as Drew was admitted to the ICU. We were met by a cluster of doctors and nurses, eerily similar to when we first arrived in the ER all those months ago, but everyone was moving faster and everything seemed more urgent. I didn't understand what was happening and was terrified out of my mind. *What was happening?* I felt like I was screaming that question and no one could hear me. I couldn't believe I nearly debated keeping him home earlier that day.

Chapter 26

Unexpectedly, Drew suddenly became ill yesterday. It progressed very quickly, but we fortunately took him to Children's early yesterday afternoon. His condition has worsened and he's currently on a ventilator in the ICU. We are struggling with this terribly and ask only for prayers at this time. Our older boys are aware, but don't have a great understanding of how serious this is. Pete will be bringing them here tonight. We are not allowed to have our cell phones on in the unit and truthfully, it's too difficult to talk right now. Please keep Drew in your prayers today. We truly believe that's what has carried us along with the incredible care he has received here. Right now, we are relying on you and the doctors here to find out what's wrong and fix it. We will update as we can.

Thank you,
Team D'Auteuil

Grief is all consuming. It eats you alive from the inside out and causes real physical pain. How did this happen? What was wrong with Drew? We had no answers yet and we were totally helpless and this had happened in just hours. Here was our little boy, hooked up to life support, tubes and wires everywhere, medications for every conceivable type of infection flowing and still he worsened. How could this have happened so fast? The doctors, gentle as they were, were very honest. The situation was very dire. Drew was in critical condition and it would be a few more hours before the tentative diagnosis of Idiopathic Pneumonitis Syndrome (IPS), with resulting Acute Respiratory Distress Syndrome (ARDS) was made. His lungs were injured by an unknown entity, probably a virus that started his cough. As a result, his lung tissue inflamed and hardened, making breathing difficult. As nearly every organ in the human body relies on each other, the damage to his lungs was a catalyst and he was now in multi-organ failure and recovery was not predicted or likely. We were devastated.

Chapter 27

Tuesday, April 13, 2010 6:11 PM, EDT

We do not have much more to tell you. Drew's condition worsened a little last night and he remains in critical condition, although stable today. Drew is being followed by BMT, ICU, nephrology, pulmonary and infectious disease doctors. Test results so far have all been negative but there are still some pending. The general talk is that Drew likely has ARDS (acute respiratory distress syndrome) without an identifiable source. We have also been told that we are on a day-to-day basis now. The doctors offer some confidence that they can support him but cannot offer any guarantees.

We are struggling still and plead for your prayers. Today, Drew had some moments of more alertness, nodded his head appropriately and even mouthed that he loved me too. It's almost impossible to believe that Drew was biking with Zach on Saturday afternoon and all this happened less than 24 hours later.

Please keep up all the prayers. We are struggling to accept that Drew could have come so far in fighting his illness to have to face this now. We know that the boy who was born smiling is a true fighter and we talk to him all day about the beach this summer, riding bikes, seeing his friends and playing soccer. Please also pray for the best doctors in the world that they will be able to help Drew get past this setback. We were so spoiled by his success the last four months that we never saw this coming and don't know how to handle it now except to pray that God helps him through this.

Thank you,
Proud Family of Andrew Liam D'Auteuil

We had the best of the best caring for Drew. Doctors from so many specialties were consulted and it was difficult to even attempt to keep track through our tears. We were told of every update, every change in medication, vent setting and lab work. Drew's care was incredible. Despite not being on service at that time, Alli visited us daily and checked in on the rounds as she could. Dr. Duncan spent quite a bit of time with us as well. As difficult as it must have been for them, they offered us no false hope.

On Tuesday evening, April 13th, our pastor, Fr. Aggie, came in to see Drew and perform the anointing of the sick. My brother John brought the twins in to see Drew. We prepped the twins as best we could in the family waiting room, but seeing their little brother like that was brutal; their emotional response was visceral and anguished. I didn't hold back my tears from them. They needed to see me cry too and realize that it was OK. I prayed relentlessly still. I never let out of my hands my paternal grandfather's rosary case. It had traveled with both my brothers John and Chris on their respective tours in the Middle East and brought them home safely. I hovered over Drew, kissed his forehead from behind the head of the bed because it was the only place that I could easily lean over all the entrapment of his lines and wires and meet untouched skin. I refused to leave his side. There was one early morning when they were taking a chest X-ray that I walked down to the chapel in the hospital at about 4 AM. I sobbed, pleaded and prayed to spare my little boy this pain, this awful insult to his recovery and to please let him heal. I texted my friend Jen Thibeault, more out of desperation to "hear" someone's voice outside the ICU and was not shocked when she answered me. She was there and listening, even at 4 AM. I couldn't call her, I couldn't speak. The sobbing wouldn't allow it. After a few texts, I returned upstairs to be with Drew, comforted only a little to know that someone in the outside world had heard me and I could count on her. Now, I had to hope that God heard me too.

Chapter 28

Wednesday, April 14, 2010 9:36 PM, EDT

Drew is still in critical condition. We are still struggling to accept that this has happened. Although there were some lab values that improved overnight, his lung function remains the same. The improvement in his labs initially sent us soaring with relief, but it's Drew's lungs that have received the severe injury and that's what the doctors are focusing on. The doctors are encouraged that his lungs have not worsened and we are holding onto that. Staying stable is the hope right now with improvement hopefully soon. Drew started treatment for ARDS with two medications last night. The tests continue to trickle in as negative for infectious disease but there are still some pending, but unlikely to be positive.

Drew has the advantage of being young and healthy prior to his transplant and even being generally very healthy even post transplant. We are praying hourly that that his youth and health, along with prayer and the amazing doctors who are doing everything they can for him, can carry him through this. The severity of this is extremely painful to us and only made worse that we are not subjected to Drew's constant stream of laughter and chatter that usually accompanied trips to Boston for the last ten months. They are sedating him a little more in order to help his lungs to rest but he still responds to us when we talk to him.

Many of the people that we have met on this journey have stopped by the ICU to see Drew including Frannie, Lori and Kadiesha from the CAT/ CR, Nuessa and Caroline from 6W, Joanie and Brianna from 6E. Of course, his much-loved primary care doctor Alli has also been a regular visitor. The transplant world is actually quite small and word about Drew spread quickly. The support from everyone at the hospital is amazing.

We don't know how to thank everyone for your prayers but ask that you please continue them. We believe they have helped Drew stabilize and pray along with you that they eventually help see him through this. We will try to update every day but please be patient with us. They have told us again that it's one day at a time and tonight we will pray for tomorrow.

Thank you,
Proud Family of Andrew Liam D'Auteuil

The thing I remember the most is how mentally and physically, I refused to let the thought of losing him into my brain. Most of my emotional struggle, besides seeing my little boy like this, was the battle of wills going on inside my brain. It as a physically exhausting battle. I was not going to accept defeat. Not now. I was living in denial town and had no intention of leaving it. The prayers to please let the doctors fix him and let us bring him home were nonstop. I only interrupted them when I had to speak to someone. Almost daily, packages and mail arrived. Anonymously, a hand crocheted prayer angel was sent to us. Pete attached Poppa's crucifix to it and then pinned it to Drew's pillow. My fellow AA moms continually sent messages and all over the U.S., Drew was on prayer chains. People we didn't even know sent messages and cards. I also knew why all the nurses and staff were stopping by to see Drew. They recognized this for what it was and came to offer their support to us. The Core medical Group sent him "Champ," a personally-designed stuffed dragon dressed up in Red Sox gear. Drew was a champ. He had been fighting for over ten months and I refused to accept that this would defeat him. It just wasn't fair.

Every doctor that entered our room, I would ask, beg and plead for them to tell me that Drew would get through this. They couldn't tell me that. I begged for any glimmer of hope, anything to tell me that Drew would come out of this. But when one of Drew's doctors asked me outright "Do you believe in God?" I answered "yes" without hesitation. She responded by saying, "Then pray, because he's in God's hands now." I physically felt my heart break.

On Friday evening, April 16th, with no improvement and what little hope we had fading with each day, the doctors told us that they would like to have Drew undergo a lung biopsy. When most people think of a biopsy, they think of a needle and local anesthetic. Not so with a lung biopsy. It was a major surgical procedure and had its risks with healthy patients. The doctors told us that they believed that this procedure only had about a 5% chance of yielding any useful information, as all of the studies and cultures to date had been negative, but they were running out of options for treatment. They were hitting him with all they had and he wasn't improving and in time, would only continue to worsen. That evening, a surgeon came to speak to us. He was very considerate to our fragile emotional state and helped us to understand the procedure and the risks. He was also quite honest that this procedure would probably cause his already critical condition to spiral. Pete and I stayed up all night, crying and discussing it and for the first time since this journey began, decided that we would refuse the recommendation of his doctors. We fully trusted these doctors to take care of Drew, but we just didn't see the point. If it would only have a 5% chance of getting any useful information and would only cause him to worsen, why would we? Besides, the only thing worse than they way he was, we couldn't bear to think about.

Early that morning, bleary eyed, exhausted and consumed by grief and the burden of the decision we were making, we anxiously awaited the arrival of the doctors to tell them that we were not going to consent to the procedure. We were approaching accepting defeat, we were grief stricken and the pain of my broken heart wouldn't allow me to take a full breath or speak fluently. Instead, the same surgeon entered our room with a big smile. My first impulse was to scream at him and lunge, fists extended. Did he just hear a joke on his way into the room and didn't manage to erase his smile before entering?? What the hell? How could he come in here smiling! Then, as my anger tuned to confusion, with that same smile he told us how he had to ask the resident to make sure that Drew's chest X-ray from that morning was actually his and not accidentally mixed up with someone else's. As we sat there dumbstruck and not sure where he was going with this, he continued to tell us that Drew's lung function had improved so much overnight that he was not recommending the surgery anymore! He had wanted to come in to tell us before he left to go talk to the rounding doctors.

We watched him leave, confused and bewildered. That surgeon wasn't even supposed to be on this morning, but he came in to tell us this news, then left us before we could say anything. We sat there perplexed, waiting for the rounding doctors to come and talk to us. We didn't dare move or think too much. I took a painful, ragged breath and held it. When the doctors arrived, they told us they took a vote. The biopsy was a no-go. I felt like I got the wind knocked out of me. What had just happened? Had God answered my nonstop praying? It sure looked like it to me.

Chapter 29

Saturday, April 17, 2010 6:36 PM, EDT

Thank you everyone for prayers and please keep them coming. We were finally allowed our first day of relief today. Drew is officially improving. Everything that happened the first few days is too much to think or write about. Maybe someday. Right now, we are just so happy to have a bit of optimistic news.

We are so grateful to Children's. When Drew's condition worsened so quickly, they acted immediately and we'll always be grateful. The response to his situation and the different specialties that came to evaluate him and offer assistance contributed to where he is at today...and that's improving. Drew was given a drug that has shown some promising results in post transplant kids who suffer the same illness and Drew's team acted quickly to get it started.

We realize that we have a long road of recovery ahead of us and there are still risks of complications. We will likely never know what triggered this illness in Drew and it's likely that even knowing wouldn't have changed the course or the treatment. What we do know is that in addition to the amazing doctors, nurses and staff here, the power of prayer is a mighty thing and no doubt played a huge role in Drew's improvement. Please continue to pray for Drew's recovery. He is still ventilator dependent and they are now slowly trying to wean him off it. There is no prediction about time...it could be days or longer before he's able to be without it.

Until then, thank you everyone for the postings and words of support and caring. Most of all, thank you for believing. It's hard for us to imagine going through this without faith. It carries you when you think you cannot stand on your own.

Gratefully always,
Team D'Auteuil

The next day, Drew's condition had improved even more. Overnight, they were able to decrease his ventilator settings even more. That morning was the first time since the first terrible day in the ICU that we attended the doctors' rounds outside Drew's room. Together, led by the Chief of the ICU, the doctors told us that they didn't know why Drew had improved so much, but they didn't care either. They expected that he could be ventilator dependent for quite a while, but were very surprised and pleased, and (once again, that phrase) cautiously optimistic about his future now. His improvement was dramatic and unexpected, but we still had to be realistic. I was even hesitant about posting that last blog for fear that this unexpected improvement might be short-lived. I remained at Drew's bedside, ever vigilant for any sign of that.

Chapter 30

Monday, April 19, 2010 3:18 PM, EDT

PRAISING GOD, THANKING CHILDREN'S AND ALL OF YOU FROM ROOM 16 ICU: Drew was extubated at about 11 AM this morning. Believe it or not, this joyous event was very nerve-wracking for us. We had just adjusted to him being stable and improving on the vent. The change was anxiety provoking. However, Drew is off the vent, still on oxygen but doing very well. The doctors are very pleased with his progress and rapid improvement, something they say is extremely unusual for someone with ARDS or IPS (idiopathic pneumonitis syndrome). They told us at rounds this morning that they don't care why he's improved so much and so fast, they're just so glad he has. So are we. The last week has been excruciating and exhausting. We still believe, in addition to the unbelievable care he has received, that it was the prayers. There's no other answer and no other explanation that would matter to us.

Drew will likely remain under close observation in the ICU for another day or two, maybe longer, maybe less. He's been taking ice chips and complaining about not being able to eat. He misses his beloved Ginger and wishes he was at home. He has essentially "lost" the last nine days and is confused about the time of day and even the season (he was telling me what he wanted to be for Halloween earlier). In addition to being intubated in the ICU for nine days, it's likely the meds that he's still weaning off of to blame for most of the fogginess and confusion.

The BMT doctors came to talk to us today. We will be in close touch with them while he's still admitted. Drew started on a med that will be given twice a week for four weeks. He's already completed the first week. He'll also be back on steroids. He will begin to wean off those in the next week or so. In all reality, the team spoke to us frankly and said that this episode has essentially set us back about three to four months in Drew's recovery. The discussion was somewhat depressing, but first and foremost in our minds is that Drew has defied astronomical odds in the most extreme challenge he's had to face yet. There is no concrete medical explanation for why that happened so we have to console ourselves that a few months' extra recovery is okay. Still, it's tough to think about going backward. However, Drew has prevailed before and will again. We had thought we were past the worst part of recovery and we let our guard down. The doctors have emphasized that there was nothing we did or didn't do to prevent this from happening, but it doesn't really stop the thought process and for us to frantically search our minds for something we must have missed or think that we failed to be appropriately grateful for. We're moving beyond that to just getting Drew healthy and home again. As for the delayed recovery now, we'll just take it one day at a time. We're definitely not going to take for granted anymore the seemingly incredible recovery that Drew enjoyed before this happened.

This has been a long nine days and we still have a while before we're home. Thank you to everyone for prayers and support. We humbly ask that you continue to pray for Drew as we're not completely out of the woods yet, but the clearing is ahead. We will probably always question why Drew had to go through this ordeal. We will never understand why it had to happen. To even imagine watching your child go through something like this is not what goes through your mind when you bring home a beautiful, healthy newborn. We are definitely scarred by this recent challenge and need to recharge ourselves to get Drew healthy, home and back on the road to recovery. We are so grateful to family and friends who have carried us the last nine days and we know will continue to carry us. Your support, love and prayers will never be forgotten.

Most of all, thank you to the most Divine Physician. We know we will be thanking God every day for this amazing intervention that the most brilliant minds in pediatric medicine cannot explain. We don't need them to.

In gratitude,
Team D'Auteuil for Andrew Liam

Nine days. Nine days of hell on earth. Nine days of refusing to accept what was happening. Nine days of incessant praying. Drew had done it. The boy who was born smiling had defied the odds and survived. Not only did he defy expectations, he did so in an accelerated manner that was perplexing and inconceivable. God heard me and answered. I had just witnessed a miracle.

Part II

Chapter 31
The Recovery Begins

Merriam Webster's dictionary defines miracle as " an extraordinary event manifesting divine intervention in human affairs." We were still coming to terms with Drew's extraordinary recovery and were painfully afraid that at any time, this incredible event might be somehow taken away from us, that it was some kind of mirage and not altogether real despite the multiple doctors and nurses who praised his miraculous recovery. Since Drew's unbelievable improvement in lung function overnight on Friday the 16th, it took him only 48 hours to improve enough to be extubated - something the doctors predicted could possibly take up to several weeks. I felt like I was walking in a fog and was traumatized beyond comprehension. My fear that the ARDS/IPS would return or relapse, something that we were told was not upheld in studies, was present every waking moment in my mind. I also knew that there aren't many studies to support relapse because they need to have enough cases of kids who *survive* to support an actual study. I was on autopilot. Take care of Drew and thank God. I barely did anything else.

The next few weeks were difficult, despite our relief and joy. Drew essentially had to learn how to walk again, with the help of a physical therapist and eventually a walker. His poor body took a horrible beating, much worse than the beating chemo and radiation had given him. In addition to his weakened state, he was still confused, time disoriented, and emotional as a result. It was amazing that my own heart could continue to pump blood with the emotional hands squeezing the life out of it. I thought I was a nervous wreck before…that was nothing. Drew was homesick and couldn't understand what we were talking about when we would try again to explain why he was in the hospital. His last memory was of biking with Zach. He couldn't remember me taking him to the ER or being admitted and watching a movie in his room that evening. It was probably for the best anyway. I would have given anything to forget those nine days too.

Taking Drew home in early May was terrifying. I couldn't explain it at the time of his discharge, but I was very uncomfortable taking him home. My anxiety was palpable. My gut was in hyperactive mode and something just didn't feel right, but I had no physical evidence to back up my instinct so I just kept it to myself. I tried to believe that it was simply just my fear of taking him outside the safety zone of Children's Hospital. Home was now a hostile environment without doctors or nurses. It would be just us. I didn't trust myself anymore to recognize danger approaching. I almost didn't bring him in last month. If he so much as developed a hangnail, I would be back.

However, my mother's intuition was correct and within just a few days of bringing him home, we were back at Children's, Drew a sickly shade of yellow. This must have been what I was sensing. Drew had started vomiting more frequently and was in pain. His gallbladder was blocked and it was backing up into his liver, making him jaundiced and in his weakened state, this condition could become very dangerous. *Not again?* Hadn't he just been through enough? A surgeon was called to put in a stent in the duct, or channel between the gallbladder and liver, to keep it open. It was a difficult and risky procedure. They told us frankly that they were concerned about Drew undergoing surgery in his still-fragile state, but there really wasn't another option. His lungs were still healing from that traumatic illness last month and the doctors were concerned about him coming off anesthesia and warned us that it could be problematic. Problematic? I was robotic and still on autopilot. This was so unfair, *UNFAIR!*

The morning that surgery was scheduled, again frantically fitting praying in between consults, while clutching my grandfather's rosary case and hoping that my lifetime's worth of prayerful requests hadn't run out, just ½ hour before he was due to be in the OR, Drew's labs from that morning came back. His bilirubin level, which monitors how well his gallbladder was working, had plummeted again to near normal levels and the surgery was cancelled. Fortunately, I was sitting down when they told me so that the staff didn't have to write up an injury report as a result of my hitting the floor. I felt a faint déjà vu to the previous gallbladder problem, which resolved spontaneously, too. I didn't know if I could keep up with the repeated skyrocketing of stress and freefalling relief when Drew bounced back again. The Comeback Kid did it again. I could literally feel my hair starting to turn gray, but I was once again so unbelievably grateful, my fingers cramped from clutching the rosary case so tightly. Someone was watching over this boy.

Chapter 32

Saturday, May 8, 2010 2:44 PM, EDT

STILL HOME: *It's a rainy Saturday, but we're still home. Drew had his clinic visit with Alli yesterday and aside from some med adjustments, it went well. The only catch is his lab value that indicates how well his gallbladder is working was up a couple of points. That could be just that he's started to eat again and the gallbladder is responding. Unfortunately, we know that this is a "wait and see" situation. We're still hoping that Drew's gallbladder will lie low until it can be removed safely. In the meantime, Drew's following a low-fat diet and all our fingers are crossed. We will be returning to Jimmy Fund on Tuesday to recheck his labs and hopefully will see some stable results, if not improving ones. If his symptoms return, then it's more definite that he will need the stent procedure that he managed to avoid last week.*

On Thursday, Drew met his physical therapist, also named Alli, who will be working with him once a week in our home to improve his conditioning, strength and endurance. Drew's not exactly happy about it, but it's another way to get closer to riding his bike again and swimming in the pool once summer arrives. We continue to see Drew's strength improve daily and that's very reassuring to see. He's definitely happy to be home and looks forward to starting school again next week with Amanda and hopefully to see some friends soon.

In just three weeks, it will mark one year that Drew was diagnosed. Last year, we went on vacation in April, enjoyed having friends over on Memorial Day weekend and we were looking forward to Drew's Fond Farewell from fourth grade and the twin's graduation from eighth grade. We had plans for summer and had been juggling carpooling for Drew's travel soccer, Ryan's school baseball team and Kevin's travel lacrosse like seasoned sports parents. It was a summer of anticipated change since Drew would be attending the middle school and the twins would be attending the high school. Less than a week later, everything changed and it's still ongoing.

We've lost the sense of stability that we had shortly after Drew's 100 days. The doctors are so reassuring that we will get that back and we look forward to it. Everything that we had to deal with in the last year was small in comparison to everything that has happened in the last month. We are about six weeks behind schedule for the completion of Drew's treatment and eventual cure. It's hard to be patient when you realize the one-year mark of diagnosis is right around the corner and we're still more than six months away from completion of treatment. Still, nothing to do but go forward from here.

So, I feel that anniversary is a word used to describe a day of honor, something worthy of remembering. I don't plan on honoring the one-year mark in June. I plan on honoring day 365 in November of this year. That will be a day well worth celebrating. Today marks day 170, almost halfway there. Until that time, we're continuing to be cautious and taking one day at a time.

To all the moms in our friends and family, Happy Mother's Day tomorrow. A special Happy Mother's Day to all my AA moms. A very special Happy Mother's Day to Aunty Dayna, for all that you do.

Thank you,
Team D'Auteuil

We continued to be at home, the days interrupted only by frequent visits to the Jimmy Fund. Drew had many more meds than before, in addition to his frequent physical therapy sessions. We were much busier than when Drew first came home after transplant and as a result, our days went by quicker, at least for me. I had to put up a chart to keep track of his medications and I was giving him his IV treatments myself. Drew also still needed help getting up and down stairs and around the house. He had to use a shower chair and I had to wrap his PICC line before he showered and flush it several times a day to keep it patent. Every night, having given up sleep as a luxury I could no longer afford, I would hover over Drew, clean the house repeatedly, all while keeping up the same series of prayers to please let my boy heal and thanking God over and over again. You would think that such a miraculous recovery would have you relieved and restful. Not so much. Your strength feels drained, your energy tapped and fatigue is chronic. Drew's doctors praised his remarkable and miraculous recovery every time we entered the clinic. I kept thinking to myself, I should be jumping for joy. Make no mistake…I was beyond grateful and thrilled, but I was also terrified. I had experienced teetering on the brink. I was terrified it would revisit.

Chapter 33

THE SUN WILL COME OUT...TOMORROW: And it did! This song was in my head yesterday as I watched the intermittent torrential downpours that we had on and off. I was happy for the rain for a couple reasons. One, our lawn was starting to fade a little and really needed it. Two, being forced inside gave me no excuse to not sit at my desk and get my checkbook in order, one of my more favorite tasks. It also helped that there was a "Law & Order" marathon on TV, so that was playing in the background as I trudged through my paperwork.

This past week, the optimism that is expressed in my lead-in has continued. We had a great visit with Alli last Friday at the Jimmy Fund with all blood counts unbelievably normal! Drew felt great last week and so far this week. His only complaint remains the new head full of curls that he's sporting. Speaking of "Annie," when you're trying to picture Drew with his new look, think "Little Orphan Andrew." Fits him to a tee. He's still plastering the curls down as best he can but the humidity last week didn't help him out any.

While I was listening to "Law & Order" and cleaning off my desk, I started to enter my receipts onto the computer. It wasn't until I came across a receipt for April 11th that my heart started to pound. There weren't many receipts for that week other than gas or parking, but it was amazing what these little slips of paper did to my heart rate. It wasn't until I started seeing the receipts for after April 21st that it started to slow down. Those receipts were "happy" receipts: picking up Drew's favorite flavor Gatorade because the hospital ran out (the nerve) or fruit cups because the hospital's were "disgusting." Increased parking slips showing that Pete or I were starting to alternate going home to be with the twins. It was like reliving it for a short while but with the wonderful outcome reinforced for me by something as silly as receipts. Life's reminders come in all shapes and sizes.

As I looked through the receipts, it was also like a mini-series that depicted hospital life through the eyes of the parent. I call it "Children's Hospital

Syndrome." For example, did you know that calories don't count when your child is in the hospital? That is evidenced by the many receipts showing bags of Dove Chocolates that have been purchased. Also, it's hard to read a book while you're in the hospital because of the constant series of interruptions that occur. Instead, the receipts showing People Magazine and other nonsense gossip mags that I wouldn't otherwise purchase were also listed. Since the magazines don't have chapters or sequels, it's much easier to pick them up and down multiple times and never lose your place. How embarrassing. Speaking of embarrassing, I wouldn't go out to my mailbox without getting dressed and at least a touch of make up on, but I have no problem roaming the halls of Children's essentially in my pajamas and no make-up. A couple of times, I have roamed to the cafe to get breakfast and that's something in and of itself. Suffice to say, if you want to eat healthy, don't eat at a hospital cafe. Now, that's not entirely true...there are plenty of healthy choices. It just amazed me how many unhealthy choices there were as well. I started daydreaming about setting up a new station in the cafe that included an EKG counter, cardiac blood tests, blood pressure screenings, cholesterol meds and instead of little packets of salt, pepper and sugar there were individual packets of Prilosec and Nitroglycerin. Oh, and a paramedic on standby.

All in all, it was a good week. We're keeping with the one-day-at-a-time pace and are hopeful that this week is also a good one. Drew has 2 ½ weeks left of steroids and then will begin his immunosuppressant wean. At that time, it's thought that he should be able to get his PICC line out. I'm not planning that far ahead. Easier to get past Friday, go through the weekend and look forward to seeing Alli again on Friday. Our weeks are going quickly and we cling to the hope of recovery and happiness once again.

Thank you to everyone who continues to follow us in this journey that we never asked for. There are many amazing things that we have witnessed and many amazing people we have met along the way. Drew is truly a soldier who makes us proud every day to be members of his army.

"But I trust in your unfailing love; my heart rejoices in your salvation." Psalm 13:5 (NIV)

Gratefully always,
Team D'Auteuil

My chronic fatigue as a result of not sleeping continued, but as evidenced in my above posting, I was beginning to feel recharged as Drew continued to improve. My faith had never relented, but I was scared to the core after

Drew's ARDS/IPS and faith or not, I was terrified and deeply scarred. I thought I had been stressed just with the illness and BMT. I didn't know what stress was until this happened. But, I was beginning to come around and with acceptance of the illness and the recognition of his amazing recovery, kept prompting a question to surface and that was "why." Not "why" in the sense of being disappointed with an outcome, but just "why?" Drew had recovered from something so devastating that couldn't be fully explained by science. Without a doubt, the doctors, nurses and respiratory therapists were incredible and Drew's care was of the highest standard. Physically, he could not have been in better hands. But that still didn't explain why he recovered. I put up a wall, pushing that thought to the other side. Drew was home. He was recovering. I shouldn't be thinking like that. I adamantly beat the thought down and aimed to focus on each day, one day at a time, grateful that my son has survived. Why did I want to dissect why he had survived?

Chapter 34

Friday, July 2, 2010 2:23 PM, EDT

I'LL NEVER LEARN... to leave well-enough alone: Even though I'm not of a suspicious nature, I feel like I never should have posted that update a few days ago. We are back at Children's. Drew was having some respiratory symptoms on Wednesday night/Thursday morning. Due to his history, Alli thought it best for him to be seen at the Jimmy Fund. There were some changes on his chest X-ray and later that afternoon, we found ourselves back on 6W at Children's.

Drew feels pretty good and looks pretty good too. His symptoms are primarily when he's sleeping. He still has a lingering cough though and his oxygen gets a little lower with exertion. Today, an echocardiogram ruled out any concerns about his heart (big sigh of relief). As soon as radiology calls for him, Drew will be having a CAT scan of his lungs. The doctors have a few ideas swirling about his nighttime symptoms, but nothing that is definite. Seeing the CAT scan could help eliminate or confirm some of these ideas. We're just hoping the CAT scan is normal and this is just residual fall-out from the cold symptoms that Drew and the rest of us had 2-3 weeks ago. Too soon to know.

Thank you for prayers and support. We will update soon.

Team D'Auteuil

On my nightly watch, I could hear that Drew's breathing was...off. It wasn't normal. He was restless, seemed to pause in his breathing too frequently and often woke up when I entered his room. It was like he wasn't reaching a deep sleep. My gut instinct's red flag went up. I called as soon as he was up in the morning, even though he looked OK. He was eating his cereal when the on-call doctor returned my page and suggested that we come to the ER. This time, I didn't debate it. I was starting to feel a familiar dreaded fear that I hoped would never return.

We weren't in the hospital long when Drew had another CAT scan of his lungs. Afterward, the BMT doctor sat down with us and told us that his CAT looked suspiciously like it did on April 10th. I couldn't believe it. AGAIN? This can't be happening. We were told that a relapse was not likely, but here we were.

At a meeting a little later with the BMT doctors, they tried to reassure us that this time they were hopeful it would be different. We were here quicker. I had noticed something and acted fast and now he was in the best place to deal with it. As much as I appreciated it, it didn't make me feel any better. There were also questions about different lung disorders and complications that can occur with transplant, and although they all agreed those disorders weren't likely, they were working to rule them out, too. There were so many doctors conferring about Drew and at the conclusion of the meeting, they told us that what they'd like to do as soon as possible was a lung biopsy. My head was roaring and the room was spinning. Here we go again....

Chapter 35

Saturday, July 3, 2010 10:49 AM, EDT

PRAYER REQUEST (AGAIN): Drew has been diagnosed with a bilateral pneumonia by CAT scan. As a result, the doctors are rallying and bringing out the big guns. He is already receiving antibiotics, antivirals and antifungals. He is scheduled for a bronchoscopy and likely a biopsy at the same time.

Our fear level is skyrocketing as many of the words and phrases we're hearing are familiar back to April. Drew doesn't remember how sick he was in April, but we do. Research and literature doesn't support the return of ARDS or IPS but we're scared anyway. Drew is nervous, too, but is easily distracted by the staff or the movies that he's been watching. The surgeons were in this morning to evaluate him and were pleased with how he looks. They will consult with pulmonary and the bone marrow team and continue to work on Drew's plan of care. In the meantime, we continue to be fearful.

Please pray for Drew's safety during these two potentially dangerous procedures and that we are rewarded with results that may help the team treat him more effectively. We are grateful for your prayers and support and ask for them once again. It's been a long year and it keeps getting longer. The fact that we are spending our second 4th of July here at Children's doesn't help either.

We will update when we can. Thank you for all your support and prayers this last year.

Team D'Auteuil

This was the procedure that we were going to refuse in the ICU before Drew's miraculous healing of his lungs occurred. To agree to it now seemed wrong and confusing. We didn't want this before! Wouldn't it make him worse again? We asked this question, but the doctors were confident that Drew would do better because he was clinically much more stable and not on life-support like before. Wonderful. He's not on life support...yet. That's all I could think about. *Yet.* By now, we realized that Drew followed no rule book for his post BMT recovery and in some ways that was good, but it also made him unpredictable. It took a long time and many questions fired rapidly at the doctors before we could agree. We were still terrified but their argument was solid and we trusted them implicitly. We just didn't like it. Drew continued to happily watch movies and read in his room. By now, he was so used to hospital life that it didn't seem to phase him anymore. He told us that he was a little nervous, but after his talk with the doctors, he seemed fine. If he was ever afraid, he never let it show. I was the one who had a hard time with that.

Chapter 36

Sunday, July 4, 2010 2:04 PM, EDT

Good Afternoon and Happy Fourth of July!

    On behalf of Team D'Auteuil, we are pleased to be able to make the following report from Jen this afternoon.

    Drew's chest X-ray looks good, and they are waiting for the surgeons to come and remove the chest tube, earlier than expected. They are also hoping to move Drew out of ICU later on this afternoon. There are still no pathology reports yet after yesterday's procedure; however, they are pleased at how good he looks!

    Our writing is not nearly as eloquent as Jen's or Pete's, but we are more than happy to be able to write such a great report on their behalf!

    Enjoy this hot day, stay safe, and keep praying for our dear friends.… May this be the LAST 4th of July that they spend at Children's Hospital!!

                                               Respectfully,

                                             The Thibeaults

The Comeback Kid was back! Drew did so well after this procedure that the doctors were able to extubate him sooner than expected and he was moved back to 6W earlier, too! Immense relief is like a waterfall pouring down on you…or it was the buckets of sweat that were cascading off me. He had his chest tube out earlier than expected the next day. He did far better than they expected! However, this was the first procedure that Drew physically struggled with pain. The operative site was painful. Movement of his arms made that pain worse. As always, the doctors and nurses had meds to help him feel better while he healed and made sure that smile was back. Next, we would have to wait and see if the biopsy was worth it and what they would find out when they took a look at it. Little did we know what a problem *that* would cause and what we would learn from it. As we waited, Kevin and Ryan would visit to help keep Drew company.

Kevin and Ryan taking Drew to the garden

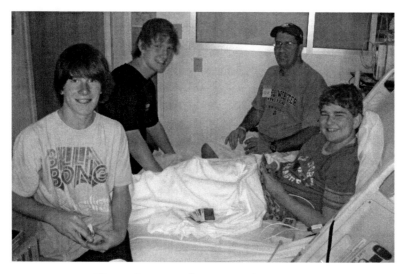

Kevin, Ryan, Dad & Drew playing Uno

That visit was one of our longest stays as we waited for the doctors to find someone, *anyone* who could actually examine and give an opinion or diagnose the biopsy results from Drew's lungs. This is when we realized even more that Drew was in a class by himself. The doctors needed someone who was familiar or specialized in lung pathology post BMT and recovered from ARDS/IPS. They couldn't find anyone. It's very possible that "The Comeback Kid" was one of a kind.

Eventually, a pathologist at Mass General Hospital felt that he could review the biopsy results and render an opinion. After getting his opinion, the doctors told us that they now believed that as a result of Drew coming off the steroids and then possibly contracting a cold, had irritated the lung tissue that had not completely healed since April. Happy 4th of July. No firecrackers and no parades, but we were celebrating another holiday, our second 4th of July, once again inside Children's Hospital. The Comeback Kid was still amazing everyone.

Chapter 37

UNCHARTED TERRITORY: *That's what Drew's doctors call his recovery since April. We have probably had the best two weeks we've had in the last 14 months. The week at the beach was wonderful and last week was full of sunshine and surprises. It's shaping up to be a beautiful Saturday, a much-needed break from the humidity, although I hear it's going to be making a comeback in another day or two. That's okay though. For the first time I can ever remember, I don't want summer to end too soon. Fall is undoubtedly my favorite time of year, but we missed all of last summer and half of this one and even if it means heat and humidity, that's okay with me. August usually signals for us the inevitable end of summer with the start of football, soccer and getting ready for school. Fall, for me, brings out thoughts of foliage, apple picking, pumpkin pie and other wonderful things that only a New England autumn can provide. I just hope that we have a beautiful, hot sunny August for Drew to swim and get stronger. But enough about that. Back to "Uncharted Territory."*

Drew had two important tests yesterday, which made for a fairly long day at the Jimmy Fund. For starters, I'm ecstatic to report that Drew's CAT scan of his lungs shows a "complete resolution of extensive pulmonary parenchymal opacities" from the June/July admission. Basically, what they believed was the IPS/ARDS making a comeback has resolved. The best news is that Drew didn't need systemic steroids to help with this. Aside from the sites where he had the biopsies and chest tube, his lungs looked wonderful. His doctors couldn't have been more pleased and Drew and I actually got a look at both CAT scan images side by side so that we could see what they were talking about.

The second test that Drew had done was the pulmonary function test or PFTs. They were essentially in the same range that they were from the last ones performed about two months ago. The results are mixed but we are reassured once again from Alli that they have many, many children who have considerably much worse scores who lead full, active lives. Even with this reassurance, I usually press for what this means for the future. That's when the term "uncharted territory" came into play. They are following Drew's recovery very closely because there are very few, if any, kids like him. I know I have mentioned that Drew will likely be mentioned (anonymously of course) in medical journals probably for decades to come. This is why it took so long to analyze his biopsy results as they searched for others to compare them to without success. So, with Alli's reassurances about his lung function and seeing Drew's stamina increasing slowly each week, we are feeling optimistic again. Given Drew's steady improvement and rock-solid lab values, they have given us two weeks off, despite my protests. They laughed. I'm not a suspicious person by nature, but every time we seem to be given a reprieve, we end up back sooner than planned. I'm really hoping and praying that's not the case this time. Drew's in a different place now and although the ultimate goal is to keep him healthy, his team feels that he's deserving of this break. I told them I'd be happy to drive him to Jimmy Fund every Friday until he graduates college if it makes me feel better, but they gently discouraged that thought. Next visit, I'm going to attempt to bargain for high school graduation then.

Last week provided many great swim days and Drew had a great time swimming with Zach T, Zach S and his buddy Tanner from Chicago (surprise #1). Then, Aunt Gail, Isabelle and Griffin came to visit on Thursday (surprise #2) and then the biggest surprise for Drew was the arrival of Uncle Chris from Texas! Surprise #3! It can be tough, as we still aren't allowed to have anyone in the house, but we made it work.

Drew, Tanner Hughes & Zach Swartz

Cousin Isabelle and Drew

Uncle Chris and Drew

Today is a day for some much needed (and probably useless) yard work. We hope to get Drew out for a long walk or maybe even ride his bike for the first time since April. We're not pushing him. I don't think it will be hot enough to swim and trust that the coming few days will provide plenty of opportunity for that. Drew has finally worked his way up to being able to hold his breath to swim underwater for short distances and that has helped his confidence tremendously. Alli has encouraged us to keep Drew as active as he tolerates and is showing steady improvement. Pete and I are working our way back to feeling the optimism that we had back the end of March and a little less of the sting that was April.

My email support group has grown and as always, please keep Drew, Ethan, Matthew, Noah, Hannah, Cody, Destiny, Preston, Jarrett and Gavin in your prayers. Especially our friend and inspiration Adam, who had his one-year "birthday" last April and has had a setback this past month. I'm thinking about him constantly and sending prayers and positive thinking his way every day. All that these kids go through…enough is enough.

Thank you for keeping tabs on us. Here's to a beautiful August.

Hopeful once again,
Team D'Auteuil

Drew, poolside with Ginger

I was still taking care of Drew as he continued healing. I was also nursing my battered heart and mind back to health and as they great stronger, the realization of what a miracle his recovery was grew more evident with each visit to the Jimmy Fund. When Alli excitedly showed us the CAT scan report stating a "complete resolution of extensive pulmonary parenchymal opacities", I was overwhelmed again. Something extraordinary happened to Drew. If he can bounce back from this, I needed to also.

The summer was going by too quickly. With permission from Alli, we took a vacation at our favorite spot, Wells Beach in Maine. We had to adhere to the same restrictions. No one could come inside the rental cottage and Drew couldn't go in any public building. You should have seen me cleaning it before I even allowed him inside. Still, it was a vacation and we were thrilled. Drew wasn't allowed to swim in public swimming pools, lakes or ponds but he could swim in the ocean. There's something about the beach that is freeing...the salty air and sound of the surf. It lowers my blood pressure and eases my anxiety. I think we all needed the rest and relaxation. Fortunately, it was a beautiful week too. Life was starting to feel better again.

Poppa and Drew

Chapter 38

Friday, October 22, 2010 2:52 PM, EDT

SKIMMING THE SURFACE, Day 337: *Updating a little earlier than I thought but not for a bad reason. Today, Drew went to the Jimmy Fund to see Andrea to work on getting him ready to return to school. I had been in touch with Alli because Drew's ongoing skin issues changed course the past week with some peeling of his hands and feet. After talking to Alli, she though it was a good idea to have him seen. But before we get into that, we have lots of positive news over the last few weeks.*

A few weeks ago, Drew made a successful trek up Pack Monadnock with his physical therapist! Sort of a momentous way to complete PT. We were also able to go apple picking as a family a couple weeks ago. It was a beautiful afternoon and Drew didn't have to wear gloves like last year. As usual, my boys paid no attention to rules about climbing the trees and you can see that by Drew's new welcoming photo on the website. We have taken the kids apple picking every year since they were old enough to wrap their chubby fingers around an apple. We look forward to it every year. We also went to the Milford Pumpkin Festival, where we saw lots of friends and Drew spent some time with his buddy Max, eating deep fried oreos and walking the Haunted Trail. Thanks to help from the Fords, we were able to deliver the 26 boxes of used athletic shoes to the pick up site in Exeter. [As a family, two years before Drew's diagnosis, we started hosting a shoe collection to benefit the Nike Re-Use A Shoe program. Nike recycles the rubber souls into playing surfaces for underprivileged communities. The perfect activity for an athletic family like ours.] Drew also started an after school archery course last week and was excited to see his buddy Nick was also taking it. Drew has attended a few lunches at school outside during the nice weather and one social studies class about hunters and gatherers. We were looking forward to spending a day or two at 6ᵗʰ grade camp before the untimely cancellation due to bedbugs (yuck!). All in all, it's been a very busy October so far!

Drew and Max at Pumpkin Festival

Kevin, Drew and Ryan with boxed sneakers for Nike drive

All of us applepicking

Today, Drew had a great art project with Andrea to help him deal with his emotions about the transplant. To hear him talking to her about everything from fear to hope and then happiness was very encouraging and made me very proud of him. She then finished up with a tried-and-true-fun project of creating a volcano with vinegar and baking soda. Always a favorite! Drew also saw Alli and Dr. Lehman. The consensus was that the new peeling of the hands and feet is GVHD but they remain unworried at this time as they feel it's very localized and minimal by most standards. We will start some topicals and follow-up in a couple weeks at what would have been Drew's next scheduled visit. Still, we made it three weeks and they've largely been a really great three weeks. Drew is looking forward to some Halloween events, including going to the Village for trick or treating and some "spooky" miniature golf at Ponemah Green.

Last week, I decided to refinish our butcher-block kitchen table. The table is ten years old and the finish was already worn by the years, but the last 18 months of cleaning and antibacterial wipes did a number on it. You couldn't put homework, newspapers or paper plates on the table without ruining them because the degraded finish would cause any paper product to stick to it. Not good. So, armed with an electric sander and a can of polyurethane, I set to work. A friend asked me if I was going to "strip" the table completely. No way. I'm not that ambitious. I was just going to sand the surface down and put on a few coats of new finish. I was a little melancholy as I remembered what caused each ding, dent and mark in the table over the years. As I sanded away the remnants of permanent marker from a project Kevin made, the ballpoint pen marks that Ryan made when he tried to use the pen as a method of cutting paper years ago and the scratches Drew made when he was pretending to be an archeologist on a dig, it got me thinking. Eighteen months are passing and we've really just skimmed the surface of all that's happened. Relentless cleaning of surfaces and our hands have left us chapped and weathered, much like my table. This website, as a way to keep everyone informed of Drew's progress, only skims the surface of emotions and medical history that has happened. After all, I don't want Drew to read this one day and be horrified at how much of his personal life I shared with the world, no matter how concerned and thoughtful everyone has been. I've very slowly been removing surface reminders of the past year and a half. Although there are still paper towels in every bathroom and Purell stations throughout the house, the pink bucket of supplies that used to follow Drew everywhere has been disbanded. I'm keeping a bag of IV supplies in my basement as insurance, much like the overnight bag that remains in my closet. The IV pole has been banished along with the shower chair to the basement as well. Drew can now use adult toothbrushes but I still rotate them through the dishwasher every day. The bottom shelf of my kitchen cabinet is slowly looking more like a kitchen shelf than a pharmacy. Our second fridge in the garage holds only a few leftover cans of gingerale that we kept "just in case." I no longer have to carry a small suitcase of supplies and medications when we leave the house. The list of meds that we keep on the fridge has been reduced to only a few listings now. Small steps toward our new normal, but steps nonetheless.

As we continue the gradual clearing on the surface of unnecessary items and reminders of the past year, we shift focus to healing the mind and heart. My heart has been "stripped" of its finish and is now healing, a slow layer-by-layer of hope for the future. Just like each day that I would gently sand the new layer of polyurethane on the table to prepare for the next. A protective gloss that will improve the appearance and integrity of the table. If only it was so easy to sand and refinish a heart. But then, a heart has much more depth than a table does and it can regenerate itself. That's what I'm relying on now. The "dings, dents & marks" that were left on my heart remain, they're only cloaked now by each layer of hope, making them less palpable.

Since I was only just sanding the surface of the table, some marks I was unable to completely remove and oddly, I didn't mind that at all. Those marks are a part of our past. You can't erase the past and you can't completely cover it up either. My heart will forever be marked by watching Drew go through this, but each new finish of hope makes those marks less noticeable and more of a gentle reminder of all that has happened to help heal it.

"Above all else, guard your heart, for it is the wellspring of life." Proverbs 4:23 (NIV)

Thank you as always for following our journey,
Team D'Auteuil

Andrea was a psychologist at the Jimmy Fund and she would check in with Drew during his visits. She would play games with Drew or together they would perform science experiments, usually involving something that would make a mess and she was such a great sport about it. After going through an illness like this, she was making sure that Drew was handling everything OK. I was thrilled that the Jimmy Fund had this service for the kids. If only they had it for the parents...but really, they had already done so much. Just seeing Drew happy again was almost therapy enough for me.

My heart was healing slowly, just like Drew was. That nagging question "why," though, kept trying to resurface, but it was a gentler question now. I was more confident now in Drew's recovery, although that confidence was still somewhat brittle, but I felt like I had to explore more fully in my heart and soul to learn the answer to that question. The only partial answer I could come up with was that God wasn't finished with him yet. I didn't understand the message yet and I certainly would have appreciated a different method of delivery, but that had to be the reason. Nothing else made sense.

120

Chapter 39

Thursday, November 25, 2010 7:51 PM, EST

EVERY DAY IS THANKSGIVING DAY, **Day 372:** *Just wanted to say Happy Thanksgiving to everyone who's been following our journey. We are relieved, thankful and ecstatic to have been home for Thanksgiving! We made a quick trek over to Uncle Jay's to see family but it was too cold outside to stay for very long. Even still, we're home. We got a little nervous when we had to go back to Boston just two days ago for some more GVH issues and I even brought my suitcase, not wanting to take any chances on a possible admission (after all, there was a holiday in two days and our luck with holidays the last two years hasn't been great). Unfortunately, Drew's issues with GVH have picked up a little speed in the last couple weeks and although the team reassured us it was mild and the GVH dentist (did you ever think there was such a thing?) declared Drew's mouth symptoms "unimpressive," he did need to go back on some medication. More importantly, we're still home. He is still scheduled for parole about Christmas time though. I'll avoid the long discussion that we had about GVH with the three doctors that saw Drew, but suffice it to say, we were told that getting to this point without any GVH is uncommon. We also know that Drew is rewriting the book on recovery and doesn't tend to show the same symptoms as the majority, so they pay special attention to him. We are very grateful. We had hoped for smoother sailing from hereon in, but as long as the med is short term and Drew responds quickly, the quicker he'll be off it.*

So, after going to the Turkey Bowl this morning, watching the Patriots this afternoon, quick drive over to Uncle Jay's and then dinner, it's been a good day. Dessert will be coming soon. The past 18 months have given us reason to believe lately that every day is Thanksgiving Day. We have so much to be thankful for this year. When I was planning and preparing our meal today, I was a little remiss at the number of shortcuts I took since it was just the five of us. Normally, I would cook for about 12 every year. It just didn't seem to make any sense to cook a whole turkey so Trader Joe's ½ turkey did the trick. Trader Joe's was also kind enough to have several all natural sides that were small in proportion so that we didn't have tons of leftovers that might go to waste since I wasn't boxing them for family to take home. These shortcuts helped me to focus on just thinking about the day.

I believe that every year, I would definitely reflect on all that we had and all that I was grateful for. Never before has being thankful meant so much to me until this year. I've spent a lot of time the last few weeks really starting to process all that has happened in the last 19 months. I'm certainly not done yet and probably have a long way to go. The video was therapeutic for me in that I had to get enough courage and confidence to actually put it together and even more to share it with everyone. It was my way of working through so much that happened in such a short time, no matter how long the 19 months actually seems. It made me realize that life itself is a constant process…we are continually learning from mistakes, learning from example and making decisions that we hope are for the best. Newton's Law's of Motion say it best…"To every action, there is an equal and opposite reaction." Every choice we make, every action we take, every word we speak will affect something or someone. This can be good or bad. Life lessons come to us every day but we don't always acknowledge them. Don't take shortcuts with your life and family. Take action. If life isn't going the way you want, take action to change it. If life gives you a hurdle, take action to confront it and challenge it. Life has plenty of challenges, both big and small. It's the action that you take to overcome your hurdles that will define you, not the hurdle itself.

Wishing you all a Happy, Happy Thanksgiving and so grateful to be home.

Team D'Auteuil

Another month until freedom! Alli had give us the magic day…December 20th, 2010. Drew would officially be released from the prison that is immunosuppressed living. He would still be on parole though. There would still be some restrictions in place, but most exciting was that Drew would finally be allowed to return to school. We had made it 19 months. We could handle one more, but the anticipation was growing. I made no plans other than to mention to Pete briefly about bringing the boys with us to Drew's December visit on the 23rd and perhaps celebrate in Boston. We had tried that last year and were denied because of that Christmas Eve admission. I was afraid to try and plan it too far ahead. We had been denied too many times before. We deserved a break this year. We hadn't celebrated any holidays with family since Easter in April 2009.

Chapter 40

Reflections: *I hope you all had a wonderful holiday! I am so happy to announce that this was probably the best Christmas and New Year's EVER! Never before have we had such a reason to be thankful to be together and just enjoy ourselves. We made the most of Drew's emancipation and armed with his list of things to do, set off to enjoy the holidays. Drew's first voyage into a public place was Frederick's Pastries Shop after we bought our Christmas tree. It was a couple days before the announced emancipation, but we peeked inside and it was empty except for the employees, so we let Drew in to see the gingerbread villages from around the world. After adhering religiously to all our restrictions and rules, it felt very rebellious! It's mind-boggling to try and distinguish the difference between that Thursday and the following Sunday, only three days later...but who cares! He's free!*

On Thursday, December 23rd, we went to the Jimmy Fund as planned and then the D'Auteuils "went to town" on the city of Boston! NE Aquarium, Faneuil Hall, Quincy Market, Dick's Last Resort, Boston Common and our final destination of the day...The Prudential Center. I'll get back to that in a bit. We arrived in Boston at 8 AM and didn't get home until about 8 PM that evening. Thank you to the Curtises for remembering our Ginger and taking care of her. The Aquarium is a favorite of Drew's and it was great to finally be back there and enjoying it! Even after five days of freedom, seeing Drew in the Aquarium just blew my mind. It was finally happening. All that talk about being "free" had happened and the world was still there waiting for us. Next stop was Faneuil Hall and Quincy Market. Lunch followed at Dick's Last Resort, where we really enjoyed the buckets of food and being treated "terribly" by the staff. It was so much fun. We went to Boston Common to see the Nativity, skating pond, lights and some young man who decided to challenge the ice of the duck pond and fell through several times. We got a good laugh at his expense. (We're not cruel. He was just being stupid and trying to entertain the crowd that had gathered.)

Christmas was a wonderful time spent going to church and being with friends and family again. Returning to church as a family. Just having our loved ones in our house was an amazing feeling. My OCD has taken a dive and I'm finding myself relaxing a bit on the constant cleaning. The change in Drew now that he's free has been nothing less than awe inspiring. So much to be joyous for this Christmas. It would be hard to top this.

New Year's Eve is often a time of reflection of the past year; a time to think about changes you might want to make or goals that you set for yourself and your family. Reflecting has a bit of a different feel for me this year. In Drew's room, his dresser is a reflection of many high points of the past 20 months. Drew's image glued to a ruler that classmates took up Pack Monadnock and carried throughout Amherst Middle School during their step-up day. A lava lamp from the Bennetts that sat in his transplant room at Children's. The coveted "Turkey Bowl" helmet, signed by the Souhegan Football players of 2009. A sculpture of a bird that Drew made while on 6E and undergoing his first round of immunosuppressant chemotherapy. Patriots stickers from meeting Julian Edelman at Children's in July '09. His Patriots hat, a gift from the amazing Core Medical Group, that was signed by Coach Belichick, Tom Brady, Randy Moss and Joe Andruzzi on a hot day last summer. His medal from successfully walking the Jimmy Fund Walk, a feat that astounded his transplant team. The painted wooden snake and snowman he made while getting his transplant. Each object a reminder of something special during a difficult time.

Reflection doesn't necessarily show us a mirror image of our lives. Sometimes we can see only what we want to. That can sometimes work in our favor, like during intense times of stress, or it can work against us by refusing to accept the reflection we see and act accordingly. I learned in June 2009 how easy it was to compartmentalize my life after Drew's diagnosis and focus on only those compartments that I could handle at that time. That often left a lot of compartments neglected. I was very lucky and blessed to have friends and family who kept letting me know they were there for me, even when I was emotionally and physically unavailable. Drew's ongoing recovery has allowed me these last six months to open more of those compartments and work them back into my life. I know we have all had those New Year's resolutions that last about as long as it takes for the thought to pass through our minds. Personally, I think New Year's resolutions set you up to fail. Instead, you should you use the time to reflect and just continue to try to be your best or make gradual positive changes in your life, whether personal or professional, until you reach your goal. Trying to do it all *at once is an all-consuming task, overwhelms you until you are frustrated and quit. Drew's illness is much like a New Year's resolution. It was a problem that needed to be resolved but we couldn't just "fix" it overnight as the clock struck 12. It took time…lots of time…but we're almost there. If you think about it, our entire lives are "resolutions," or at least should be.*

Drew has started his return to school this past week and has once again amazed us with his resilience and his determination. He went to school Monday for half a day and has been attending full days since. Tomorrow is Jimmy Fund Friday, so he'll miss school but he still has Amanda on board and his teachers were prepared for him to have some work over the weekend. Alli is going to be so proud of him! He's been swimming twice now and has skied three days this past vacation with no evidence of missing an entire season. His skill and form are still great. He tires easily, but refuses to give up. Now, there's my inspiration.

When we first started our near daily treks to Boston, Drew would ask about the Prudential Building, easily visible on our way to Children's. Since he first noticed it, he has asked about going there, especially when he heard there was a restaurant on the top. This wish of his would be mentioned routinely on our trips and it was the #1 destination on Drew's list of things to do once he was off restrictions. On that evening, after our crazy, busy day in Boston, we told the host that this was a special occasion and shortly after arriving, we were seated in a corner table with a perfect view of Fenway Park…and Children's Hospital. While the boys were busy talking about and checking out Fenway, I was looking at Children's and realizing that it had finally happened…Drew made it to the Top of the Hub. Now, that's a reflection.

"What you decide on will be done, and light will shine on your ways." Job 22:28 (NIV)

Eternally grateful,
Team D'Auteuil

Between our freedom to spend the holidays with family and friends and Drew's return to school, we were the happiest we had been in 20 months! We were officially back in the world! The same world that was our enemy for so long. Drew's return to school was fairly smooth and he continued to keep Amanda as a resource since he still had many appointments and would miss a considerable amount of school. I remember vividly dropping Drew off that first day of school along with his brothers. I was starting back at my part-time job that day, too. In retrospect, I probably should have taken a few days to adjust to this new phase in our lives. As I drove out of the school parking lot, my tears fell freely. After literally hovering over my son for 20 months, protecting him from the rest of the world , I was releasing him into school, the rough equivalent of a petri dish in my mind. It was a difficult transition for me. If it was for Drew, he never showed it. The Comeback Kid walked swiftly over to the other kids gathered and disappeared in the crowd, swallowed up by normalcy. Just another middle-school kid.

All of us at the Top of the Hub. Freedom!

Chapter 41

TEARS OF A DIFFERENT COLOR: *Time for a long overdue entry. It's been tough to get to the computer for any extended period of time lately. We have been very busy and most of it has been a good busy. Drew is back at school, almost full-time except for a few visits to Boston, and is excelling academically. I'm very proud of him! Pete and I had the privilege of watching Drew recite a poem for a poetry recital last week. As my friend Kendra, who also attended, observed, I looked more nervous than Drew did. All for nothing, as he did great!! Of course, when he finished, the tears started flowing freely and without control. Drew let me know he saw me but I think he enjoyed laughing about it more than being embarrassed by it.*

Kevin and Ryan are enjoying having friends in the house again and I was privileged last week to make a Mexican feast for seven of them one evening. So much fun to have everyone in the house again! We've been free for a little over a month and are still so thrilled to have friends and family in our house again and getting out a bit. You never realize how much isolation affects you until you experience it. It's not fun but it does make you realize how much you value your friends and family and how easy it is to take your way of life for granted.

Drew is working on building up his strength and stamina and has enjoyed skiing and sledding with some buddies. His seamless return to school has amazed me so much and his attention to his school work is so impressive. Amanda definitely helped keep him in top academic shape for his return and we'll always be grateful for that. His team of teachers continues to be so supportive and the kids have welcomed him in a manner that you have to witness to believe. The middle school years are tough enough. Toss in a serious illness and long-term absence, and it could potentially be unbearable. Drew has the strength of someone way beyond his 12 years and his ability to adapt to any situation is mind-bending. We should all be so fortunate.

Drew was seen in the quarterly GVH clinic this past Monday and also saw Alli. The visit was a "good" one. I've put good in quotes because it was good, particularly in the transplant world but sometimes the translation to the "regular" world can be tough to take. Drew's GVH was fairly extensive. We were happy to hear from the doctors that day that the GVH is officially in remission. However, the symptoms will take some time to go away and flare-ups can occur for up to five years before it finally burns itself out. He also saw the GVH dentist who said that his teeth look great and his oral symptoms will also continue to calm down and eventually burn out as well. The dermatologist saw no problem with Atlantis next month, but of course, emphasized the need for sunscreen.

Drew also has a couple of appointments that would seem ordinary to most people, but they are events for us. He will be seeing his own dentist and eye doctor next month for a regular check up. This will be the first time he's seen a health-care provider outside of Children's/The Jimmy Fund. Another sign of returning to our former life. Who would have thought that I would be so happy setting up those appointments??

There have been many tears that I've shed these past 20 months. It's a good thing tear ducts don't wear out. Much like my emotions, my tears have evolved nearly full circle in this time. The dark, fearful tears in the beginning raged for many months in varying intensity, blurred my vision and were nearly impossible to control. Once we learned Drew's chemotherapy failed and he would have to have a transplant, they were more vivid with a combination of anxiety, anger and grief. After Drew's transplant appeared successful, they seemed lighter and easier to see through. The seemingly endless veil of saline over my eyes was lifting somewhat. I wouldn't walk around constantly with red, irritated eyes and white chalky trails on my face.

Just as it did in the beginning of our journey, my tears are triggered very easily as evidenced by the poetry reading. Just to see Drew, standing on the small stage, confidently reciting the poem he studied so diligently for. To see him as he should be. A regular sixth grader. It was just overwhelming. The tears were different though… lighter and brighter. I could see clearly through them. They weren't heavy and dark and they didn't burn as they flowed. They reappeared each time I told someone about Drew's successful reading. Each accomplishment he has is a reason to celebrate. If tears of happiness could be bottled and sold, I'd make a fortune. They shine brighter than tears of pain and sorrow and remind us that life is something to be celebrated. I've watched my tears transition just as our lives have. To hear Drew discussing a game he played in gym with his older brothers brought tears to my eyes as the twins recalled their own happy memories of the same. A regular sixth grader.

Of course, he's not regular. He's a walking miracle.

"Jesus looked at them and said, "With man this is impossible, but not with God; all things are possible with God." Matthew 19:26 (NIV)

Gratefully always,
Team D'Auteuil

Keeping in mind and prayers always our AA friends, Adam, Noah, Ethan, Destiny, Hannah, Jarett, Cody, Matthew, Gavin, Charlotte and most of all little Preston, who's been having a tough time lately. We're all pulling for you!

Anything is possible. Drew had proven that to us. Trying to merge back on the highway of normal life was still challenging at times and we had constant reminders that things were still different. Multiple appointments and daily medications reminded us that we weren't "normal". Drew's miracle status was still evident and "Comeback Kid" title appropriate. I never let up from constantly praying, although it felt less urgent now. I needed it more as daily strength and stamina. It kept me honest and helped me filter what was important and what wasn't. Having a sick child makes you see the world differently. Perspective is enlightenment, but that enlightenment isn't always enjoyable. Enlightenment means being aware of the full truth. Sometimes seeing that truth is painful. My view of the world had changed. I was more conscious of choosing what would be a priority each day and what would be discarded or left to wait. Being selectively reflective left me leaning on my faith even more. My fear that Drew's miracle status would somehow be revoked was ever present, but I was becoming more comfortable with the thought that something incredible had happened. In order to accept that full enlightenment of this miracle, I had to accept the trauma that led me to it. We had come to the doorstep of loss, knocked, but we were turned away. Why?

Chapter 42

Wednesday, February 16, 2011 6:37 PM, EST

SUPERSTITIONS & SKIING: *Happy Belated Valentine's Day. Not really a "holiday," but another reason to give and receive chocolate, and since they have not yet declared an official Chocoholic's Day, I'll take it.*

We had our regular Jimmy Fund Friday last week. It was a long day, but I'll get to that in a bit. Today, Pete and I took advantage of our days off and the beautiful weather to declare a "truancy" day and surprised the kids this morning with a trip to Sunapee, rather than school. It could not have been a more perfect day for skiing. We haven't skied as a family in two winters and even though we have the Make-A-Wish trip coming up shortly, we felt the strong need for a family day and so it was. We arrived shortly before 9 AM this morning and quickly made our way to the slopes. It was a great feeling to be all together skiing again. Of course, I remembered quickly as we skied together how all my boys are far superior skiers than I am! An unusual site was watching Pete take a tumble just before our first run. It was then that I said "I haven't fallen in four years." It wasn't too long after that a snowboarder decided to break my record. He was definitely one of the most polite snowboarders I've even had the misfortune to cross paths with and I believe that I heard him say "sorry" just before my legs went out from underneath me. I knew I never should have said that statement. I have an education and background based in science and a strong faith. Superstition has never been my practice, but it is amazing how a statement can entice fate to bite you for tempting it.

Keeping that in mind, Drew had a low-grade fever a week ago Monday. He knew that something was wrong and went to the nurse. I was so proud of him for recognizing when he needed to report something, and also proud that he reported it and then asked to return to class! When I received that phone call, I worked very hard to keep the panic bile from rising in my throat. I was able to suppress the panic as I reasoned that Drew was past one year BMT and this shouldn't be a big deal. I convinced myself so much that I emailed his doctor, rather than paging her. You may recall that fevers were our enemy from June to August '09. Drew had 14 admissions in 11 weeks for fevers. Many of them were in the middle of the night. Until that Monday last week, Drew had not had a fever since August '09. That was a statement I never uttered out loud. To make a long story short, Drew's doctor called me and felt that although Drew was so far out past BMT, he still should be evaluated, have labs and received a painful, horse-sized injection of an antibiotic. The good news was that everything was normal. The bad thing was Drew still had to receive the painful injection. We also learned that "stat" labs in Boston meant about 20-30 minutes. In a small NH community hospital, it meant 5½ hours. So, here I am, this person of education and faith, but for nearly 18 months, I was afraid to verbalize out loud that Drew hadn't had a fever since August of '09. Well, at least now I can put that behind me.

Drew, Ryan & Kevin at the top of Sunapee

In the meantime, Drew has been busy at school, Hampshire Hills, seeing friends, visiting Wilkins School and spending time with family last weekend when Uncle Brian, Caroline, Aunt Joanie, Uncle Sal, Jane and Cliff came to visit. We all enjoyed watching the Super Bowl (I meant the commercials, as we weren't really invested in either team) and skiing as well. Drew also is starting an interest in lacrosse and has been practicing a little bit.

Aunt Joanie and Drew playing bananagrams.

Me, Cousin Jane, Uncle Jay (background), Aunt Caroline and Uncle Brian

As for the Jimmy Fund update, not a whole lot to report there. We arrived early for lung function tests, saw Alli and ended up having an infusion of IVIG, something Drew has only had to have once since transplant. Basically, it's an immunoglobulin that helps to protect him against viruses. His level was a little *low and Alli believes that it's because he's still on steroids for his GVH. She wanted to make sure that he was covered before our trip to the Bahamas, which is good, but it made for a loooong day. We didn't get home until almost 5 PM that evening. Drew's lung functions were stable and that was a positive sign, but one part of his complete blood count dipped a little bit and that was his hemoglobin. It was only by one point but Alli attributed it to the ongoing wean of the steroids that Drew is on. We don't have a return visit until after we get back from our Make-A-Wish trip, but will get labs just before leaving and hope that they remain stable and the hemoglobin improves. It's not "low," just on the low side of normal and they don't want it to go much lower. So, the steroids continue....*

Superstitions are probably only as strong as you allow them to be. Still, they can be quite powerful. Just as faith is a confidence you develop and nurture over a lifetime, you can also be courted by the fears that surround superstitions. Superstitions are not based on logical deductions or evidence-based science. They are irrational beliefs that are based out of fear or ignorance. However, faith isn't based on science either. You just have to choose what you wish to subscribe to. Faith is based on trust and confidence that God will take care of the unknown for us. Of course, some superstitions are just silly or fun. Football players who refuse to wash their uniforms while on a winning streak, avoiding black cats and 13th floors, etc. The trick is to realize how much you want to devote to fears that have no basis in knowledge. We spent most of the last two years focused on science, statistics and facts. Mixing that with our faith has been a nice reprieve from all the data we've constantly had to process and decisions we've had to make. We still hope and pray that Drew will continue to recover uneventfully and continue to contribute to positive statistics, facts and medical journals. Better go knock wood.

Peace and Gratitude
Team D'Auteuil

Faith is what carried me, along with the support of so many. Prayer undoubtedly played the most important role in Drew's miraculous recovery. When you are constantly researching, checking stats or reading studies, especially when you're emotionally involved, it hurts your brain...and your heart. To me, it was easier to let go of the clinician in me and just give in to faith. To see Drew now, acting like a normal kid, made me smile. My daily perspective continued to dance around that persistent question of "why?" There was nothing to stop me from believing that a miracle had happened. In my heart, I already knew *why* Drew survived. There was an intervention. But if the brilliant medical team that took care of him couldn't explain it, then "how" was the question now.

Chapter 43

Written Mar 20, 2011 7:53pm

WHEN YOU WISH UPON A STAR...: *Or, if you have two of the best Wish Granters in the world, wishes do come true! Thank you to Kim and Lynda for working so hard to grant Drew's wish! But, I'll get back to that.*

The last few weeks have flown by. Drew has had a few more "firsts" of his new normal, all of them good. He had a boys' weekend, skiing with a few buddies and Dad shortly before February break. He recently had his first sleepover at a friend's house...OK, that was really a first for me as I had to let him go. I won't lie...it wasn't easy, but he was so happy that it made it hard to deny him that opportunity.

Drew has continued to do awesome in school and has been working on his new-found love for lacrosse. It looks like I'm going to have three lacrosse players in the house this spring! He's very excited and the motivation we see in him is so wonderful! His brothers have been busy giving him tips and he's spent several afternoons of our recent beautiful weather at the school and Hampshire Hills with friends playing wall ball and practicing his skills. Drew hasn't been able to play soccer for two years and witnessing him develop a love for another sport is simply awe inspiring. I've been so proud of how he's carried himself despite all he's been through. He's the toughest kid in the world to me.

We did have a quick trip to the Jimmy Fund the Friday before our trip because Drew had a slight cough. All was good and the steroid wean is back on. How he does the next few weeks will determine if it's a longer wean, but regardless, we just look forward to him being off this medication. Now, on to the best news of all.

Make-A-Wish Trip to Atlantis! Without a doubt, the best vacation we've ever had! Thank you so much to Kim, Lynda and everyone at Make A Wish and everyone who supports this unbelievable organization! From the limo ride to and from the airport, our great accommodations, amazing food, water slides and the incredible marine life, we had the most amazing time! It would be difficult to describe everything in the detail that would do it justice. Suffice it to say, it was awesome! There were endless marine-life exhibits including shark tanks and Predator Cove with tiger sharks and sting rays. We fed sea turtles and sting rays, and watched the employees feed the sharks. There was the "Dig," which was a tunnel with aquarium windows where you could see all kinds of marine life along with the "ruins" of Atlantis. We rode water bikes and kayaked in the lagoon, played ping pong by the pool, rode the lazy river too many times to count and, everyone but me, defied gravity on the "Leap of Faith" waterslide (no thanks!). We had a wonderful week without crowds and never waited in line for anything. We explored the many pool areas, the beach and other hotels. We ate in restaurants that were indescribable, toured the shops and just enjoyed ourselves thoroughly. We definitely haven't had that level of fun and relaxation in a very, very long time.

Probably our favorite thing was Dolphin Cay. As a family, we had a private encounter with two trainers and a 12-year-old dolphin named Hercules. Our welcome photo shows one of our pictures with him. It was fantastic and so unreal to be that close to such an amazing creature. The control and rapport that the trainers have with dolphins is something to witness that close up. Drew and I also had an encounter with a 375-lb. sea lion named Freebie! Believe it or not, Drew and I both agreed that as much as we loved the dolphin encounter, the sea lion encounter was even better! The only way to attempt to describe it is that the sea lion acts almost like a friendly, but very large, dog. Nuzzles you, loves to be petted and thrives on positive reinforcement. We got a tour of the facility, saw the medical lab and learned a lot about how they care for the dolphins and sea lions there. We loved it!

Start to finish, there was nothing to complain about. We will always be grateful to the Make A Wish Foundation and support them as much as we can. We know first hand that there is nothing in the world that can make up for everything that he's been through, but this was one heck of an attempt. We have thank yous to write and pictures to send to Atlantis for them to post in their newsletters and I have 712 photos to arrange into a book and that doesn't include the 134 photos from Dolphin Cay that they gave us!

I never imagined in a million years that my own child would be a Make A Wish recipient. It's surreal and humbling at the same time. Despite the time that has passed since Drew's June '09 diagnosis, there are still times that it hits me hard and takes my breath away. I would wish on a million stars to make all this go away and just give me back my healthy boy, but I know that's not going to happen. What I can do is be grateful for where we are now and how Drew has handled it. That's what I have to remind myself, every hour of every day. Drew's strength and courage would rival that of a grown man. His determination to get back into the real world and be an ordinary kid again is something to behold. I only wish I had his strength and perseverance. I'm so proud of him.

Lastly, our return trip home was on Kevin's and Ryan's 16th birthday. It wouldn't be fair to not mention how strong they have been the last two years and to say Happy Sweet 16 to my boys! They have been through their own turmoil witnessing their little brother's illness and all he's been through. I'm so proud of both of them as well! Happy, Happy Birthday!

Thank you so much for continuing to follow us on this journey. A special thank you to my wonderful friends at Dartmouth Hitchcock who compiled a cookbook in Drew's honor with proceeds going to the Jimmy Fund! Drew even illustrated the cover. The support from Drew's Army will never be forgotten!

Happy 1st day of spring to everyone! Drew has another visit to the Jimmy Fund this Friday and I hope to get another posting with positive news shortly after that. In the meantime, enjoy the sunshine and the promise of spring. I know I've been looking forward to it! We have also learned of a 13-year-old-boy named Bryce in CA who was just diagnosed with AA a few weeks ago. We're keeping him in our thoughts and prayers and will follow his journey, just as so many have followed ours. They need to know they are not alone. I don't know what I would have done without my special "AA moms" network.

Peace and gratitude,
Team D'Auteuil

I couldn't believe that I was taking Drew out of the country. Alli and his other doctors were so thrilled that we were taking this trip. It was so frightening though. I still looked at Drew as fragile, even if he was the toughest kid I knew. How could I do this? How could I take him so far away from the Jimmy Fund? We had been isolated for 20 months and had only been free for about seven weeks. It seemed a bit ambitious. All I could think about was the airplane and all that recycled air and what Drew might catch. It's hard to switch gears, but somehow I managed and we had the most wonderful week in Atlantis! I think I packed an entire suitcase with sunscreen, as Drew had to be really careful in the sun. Not only was he fair skinned, but his graft vs. host could be awakened by a sunburn, so I wasn't taking any chances. I also packed a small pharmacy of "what ifs," just to have them on hand. Don't even think I opened that bag!

To have that freedom…after so long to just be there with no worries other than making sure Drew didn't get sunburned…it was indescribable. Although I declined going down the "Leap of Faith" waterslide, I didn't miss an obvious opportunity to see that as another reminder of what we'd been through. I didn't exactly view our journey as a "leap" per say, it really felt more like a shove. On one beautiful afternoon, as I watched Drew swim with his brothers, it hit me again. Drew was a survivor. He wasn't really sick anymore. He was just facing the fallout from the treatment that cured him of his illness. A unique survivor and no one deserved this trip more than he did. I took over 900 photos and to this day, have yet to put them in an album. It's a project just too overwhelming to think about. I will someday. In the meantime, that moment of gazing into the beautiful blue sky and then seeing all my boys together, almost brought me back to a time when being a mother didn't hurt so much. I was hoping to find myself there again more frequently. Make A Wish helped me start.

Drew, Me & Freebie

All of us with Hercules

Chapter 44

ALPHABET SOUP: *We returned today from a long visit at the Jimmy Fund for the "Graft vs. Host Clinic," otherwise known as the "GVH" clinic. Sometimes, in more formal literature, it's referred to as "GVHD," as in "Graft vs. Host Disease." Any way you spell it, it's still not much fun. Since June '09, we have learned a new language of acronyms. Whether it was the illness itself (AA), tests that Drew had frequently (CBC, ANC, H&H, etc.), places we had to go to (CAT/CR, 6W) or procedures he's had done (PICC lines, BMT), we could have easily scripted a key to carry around with us to keep up with the medical alphabet soup we were drowning in. Some things even had two acronyms, like BMT (bone marrow transplant) which also has SCT (stem cell transplant) as another name. We've become quite fluent as our brains automatically process the written word as soon as our eyes register it. It's a similar process for us now with this "language." The good news is that it has evolved so well that we rarely need much translation from the doctors now, unless it's something new. Beside the obvious convenience of shortening some rather lengthy names or phrases, I think referring to something in its abbreviated form is yet another protective coping mechanism. Initials and letters sound less threatening than scary words that someone can easily misinterpret. So, today was GVH day. A new phase in this journey we continue on....*

First up was the GVH dentist, Dr. Nat. He let us know how pleased he was with Drew's oral symptoms continuing to be "unimpressive" and was happy to tell us that he didn't need to see Drew for about a year! When we first saw him back in December when Drew's symptoms were at their worst, he still reassured us that it was mild. Next up was the dermatologist, "Dr. Art." He also was very pleased with Drew's skin and has called his GVH "very mild" once again. One of the concerns we had with Drew's GVH was how much it was affecting his muscles/ligaments and would that affect his growth? The wonderful news is that it won't...IF Drew remains active. We have a whole plan in place now and have already contacted his wonderful former PT (physical therapist Allie) who was very happy to hear from us. PT Allie (not to confuse with Dr. Alli) is an avid bicyclist and lacrosse mom and since the dermatologist highly recommends biking, we were thrilled to know that she was going to help us again. The first five years of GVH are most telling...its mainly prevention status now. The more active and the more Drew grows in the next four years will help minimize more chronic problems. That brought us to our second question about Drew today...his growth.

Fortunately, we had an opportunity to sit with Drew's Dr. Alli and really get a grip on all that has been happening the last few months. Between the GVH, his high BP (blood pressure) and worry about his kidneys, we were feeling a little fragmented and frustrated about how Drew was doing in general. All things considered, the doctors are very pleased. We heard again today that considering what Drew had to overcome a year ago, they are thrilled. If his ARDS/IPS hadn't occurred, Drew's current status would still be considered about the "norm" and still mild. What Dr. Alli described as a system of peaks and valleys is par for the course of a typical BMT patient and not unexpected. We talked about Dr. Stack's (nephrology - kidneys) report and the undesired news that Drew's kidneys have been damaged. To what extent remains uncertain. At this time, they feel the damage is minimal and they hope to maintain that so that they provide a long, healthy life for him. We know that people can survive with one kidney and Alli told us that certain types of CA (cancer) treatments can reduce kidney function to less than 25%, but the kids do OK. Some kids even will see an improvement in time of up to 60% in subsequent testing. We also talked about Drew's growth, which hopefully will begin again shortly. Although Drew's illness and treatment have delayed his growth for the last two years, the doctors see no reason that he shouldn't catch up in time. This growth will also help stretch the muscles and ligaments affected by GVH.

A long day, a little emotional as we talked about the present and the future and expectations. No one can predict the future. We know what we've overcome in the past and just want to keep moving forward. It's a tremendously difficult process and very draining, something that I was very honest about in my last posting. Drew's resilience keeps us real, but even he has his moments. Today though, after our discussion, we feel like we have a better grip on the overall picture and what the doctors will be looking for in the next few visits. Drew's blood counts have been nothing less than perfect the last six weeks or so, clear evidence that despite the steroid wean, the generalized inflammation has subsided. That was exactly what the doctors were looking for. Drew continues to deliver.

So do the Red Sox! Drew was thrilled to meet Jed Lowrie at a recent visit to *the Jimmy Fund! Finally! It seemed too often that we would just miss someone by being an hour too late or a day short. Drew's URI (upper respiratory infection or "cold") visit couldn't have had better timing. It made the unexpected visit there worthwhile.*

Although I have said repeatedly that I will not honor the two year mark in just a couple of weeks, I'm sure it will not go unnoticed in my brain or heart. The last couple of months have been very frustrating and taxing. It's been a long time. Thank you to those of you who have stayed in close touch with me lately to check on Drew and lift my spirits. It helps more than you will ever know and I'll never forget it. Life is better. I'll leave it at that. It's a good day for soup…I've just always been more partial to chicken noodle.

"Whatever you decide to do will be accomplished, and light will shine on the road ahead of you." Job 22:28

Peace,
Team D'Auteuil

We were continuing our new normal and finding a rhythm that worked for us, including the every other Fridays that we would return to the Jimmy Fund. Drew remained on the hated steroids that altered his appearance and as a result, his self esteem. Corticosteroids, like Drew was taking, act as a strong anti-inflammatory in the body, which is what you need when you're fighting GVH. Unfortunately, they have some unpleasant side effects. Not only do they increase your weight, but that weight (a combination of fat and fluid) is redistributed to areas including your face, stomach and upper back. Once Drew was off them, he would slowly lose the added weight and altered appearance. However, for now he would continue to take them while his doctor tried to wean the dose lower while watching for his hemoglobin to rise, which would indicate that his GVH was finally admitting defeat. Despite his altered appearance, you would never realize this boy was self conscious. He got up every morning and went to school, oblivious. To me, he just looked like Drew, the boy who was born smiling. If the kids at school thought anything, it was never spoken. Drew was accepted, just as he was.

However, there were some new areas of worry, like his kidneys, and we were following up with nephrology, or the kidney specialists. Ever present in the back of my mind was how just a little over a year ago, Drew was in an entirely different place. We had just come home from the hospital and he was the most fragile he had ever been. It's mind bending the difference a year can make. He was now learning to play lacrosse and riding his bike again. We were looking forward to our first summer of freedom in two years and already had so many plans. I never forgot though. I never forgot to be thankful. Drew still had challenges to face, but I had to learn to see them as minimal in comparison to everything he had faced so far. Drew's initial diagnosis and subsequent BMT was the battle that lasted ten months. April 2010 was a war that lasted nine days and he emerged victorious, but terribly damaged. Each additional challenge loomed in my mind as another enemy assault. It was hard not to react to each one.

I was also coming to terms with the fact that my role as a mother was changing. My previous role, that of a relatively carefree mother of three, no longer existed and would never return. That's not pessimism, it's reality. I didn't choose this path, but I had to find a way to navigate it. Drew could potentially have more challenges to face as a BMT survivor. As Drew continued to recover, I thought more and more about what my role would evolve to. As Drew's strength increased, it fueled my desire to make something positive out of this journey. Instead of the role I never asked for…that of a mother to a sick child, a new role was emerging. A vocal role as an advocate - for AA, for the support of families affected by AA and to encourage every eligible man, woman and teen to sign up for the bone marrow registry. (www. marrow.org. Be the Match website.) We had been so blessed in many ways on this journey. It was time to think about paying it back.

There was no denying that this experience changed my life in every way imaginable. Priorities are reviewed and revised constantly. You view every aspect of daily life differently. That's not to say that I'm perfect and never react anymore over life's small aggravations. I still get annoyed by people driving slowly in the passing lane, balancing my checkbook and empty shampoo bottles in the shower. Using this journey as an excuse to transform into a bubble-headed optimist spewing sunshine would get old quickly, both for myself and the general public. I continued to use Drew's Caring Bridge site as my main therapy. I can say honestly that I never planned what I would write. That's why I never thought I could ever write by choice. When I wrote the updates, it was because something had inspired me. It might have been events that day, the latest Jimmy Fund visit, a song I heard…it could be anything. It was what was in my heart at that time and so often, I would write it to convince myself of what I was feeling. Putting it in writing made it tangible. It made it real. Maybe then I could believe it and if I could believe it, maybe someone else could feel that hope too. The fact that I would use that to put an entire book together…well…that was unexpected, but so was this journey. Life is full of surprises, some good and some not so good.

Despite my ongoing role evolution, I still continued with my daily struggle about Drew's illness and how it had affected all of us. I now had time to think about other things. I had to learn how to live our new "normal". Every day brought new challenges to that new normal. I didn't really even know what normal was anymore. I had no choice but to learn as I went along. I no longer wanted Drew's illness to define us, but I couldn't deny all the blessings that came as a result of being forced on this unwanted journey. I didn't want to keep thinking about how Drew had survived. If I thought about it, I had to remember those horrible nine days. Time had not fully healed that wound and maybe there was a reason for it. Praying that had frequently been gratitude, was leaning toward inquisitive now, but I think I was beginning to understand.

Chapter 45

Monday, July 11, 2011 6:58 PM, EDT

RENOVATIONS & REHABILITATION: *Here's hoping everyone had a wonderful 4th of July week. We absolutely did if only for the fact that we were HOME this year!! There's a milestone worth celebrating! For the first time in two years, we enjoyed the fireworks, parade, family and friends. It was an awesome way to kick off the summer and we hope that feeling continues.*

A few updates. Just before the 4th, we all enjoyed a ride on "Codzilla" in Boston. A high-speed cruise out of the Boston Harbor, courtesy of the Jimmy Fund and sponsored by the wonderful Andruzzi family and their foundation. We have been privileged to get to know the Andruzzis through their foundation and support of Children's Hospital and Dana Farber. We reap the benefits of their support of families who have been through traumatic illnesses and our boys get to say that they personally know a football great. Jennifer and Joe Andruzzi have asked us to tell our story for their foundation and it will be published and also available on their foundation website and Facebook. We felt honored to be asked and look forward to doing that soon.

The 4th of July brought our Florida family for a visit and it was a great week for us all to be together. Uncle Brian, Aunt Caroline, Jonathan, Zach, Ethan, Sam and Kyra had a great time experiencing a true New England summer and let us know that it's hotter here than in Florida. They left this morning and it's too quiet around here. I miss them all already.

Drew continues to be the toughest kid I know. He's continuing his physical therapy regimen with a great therapist, Mary. It hasn't been easy for him and at times, very frustrating. Still, he continues and last week Mary gave him the good news that his flexibility has improved in one of his most difficult areas, his ankles! It helps that he's been so active this summer and enjoying his time biking, playing lacrosse and seeing his friends at Hampshire Hills. Drew's most recent visit with Dr. Alli, now a full Attending Physician at Children's and Dana Farber

(Congratulations!), was all good news so far and Dr. Alli was able to reduce his steroids a little bit. There are still a couple of labs pending, but we're hopeful they will be good too. The day itself didn't go according to plan, but we're past that now. Drew will be seen two weeks from today in the Graft vs. Host Clinic and we hope that the doctors see some improvement as well. There are also two very important tests coming up in a few weeks that have us on edge. One is the repeat of the pulmonary function tests. The last few times, they have been stable and we're really hoping that there's some more improvement. The second is a new test for his bones. Drew's been on steroids for so long that they want to check the density of his bones. More things to worry about.

As Drew continues down his road of rehabilitation, we took note of our surroundings and decided it needed a little rehabilitation as well. Maybe renovation is a better word for it. Either way, two years of focusing on Drew has left our house somewhat neglected. Our screen porch was our first project and we set about planning and finding a contractor. The second project was our pool deck that Pete decided to tackle himself. A lot of research, a little planning, combined with some help from friends and family and we have a beautiful new deck. Simultaneously, our screened porch was reconstructed into a new three-season sunroom and the combination of the two projects makes us very happy! Something run down was converted to something beautiful and useful.

I also decided to get into the game and set about my own project of refinishing my table and chair set for the sunroom. A lot of sanding and painting later and my set looks new. It's amazing what a little elbow grease will do to a 10-year-old table set that's been battered and bruised. My arms were killing me the next day, especially from the spray painting, but it was so worth it when I looked at the results. It made me wonder what goes on in Drew's mind when he's at physical therapy and working so hard to rehabilitate his body that has also been so battered and bruised. In rehabilitation, the goal is to restore something to the optimum level of functioning. Renovation is restoring something to an earlier condition. To me, the difference is splitting semantic hairs. Renovating and rehabilitating the human body requires a similar process to a building. The doctors are the engineers who come up with a plan and the physical therapists act as the tools who mold, shape and revitalize. The only difference is that a building is an inanimate structure that cannot assist in it's own improvement. Sort of a sad irony to think that the porch and the deck had it easier than Drew does. Drew's experience has already shown us what the human body is capable of and we hope and pray that this "Rehabilitation Road" takes a turn onto "Recovery Lane" very soon. There's no GPS to show us when that will be. Our impatience continues to keep our speed at a slow pace.

However, the summer already seems to be speeding by at high velocity and I wish I could slow it down a little and enjoy every minute. I had high hopes for Drew being off steroids, weaning off his blood pressure meds and returning to school this fall as a new kid, his body reconditioned back into its former state: beautiful, perfect and useful. I wanted to see him playing soccer again with his former grace and agility. I even have gotten used to and accepted the curly hair that he likes so much. I just wanted to see what my boy looked like now as a 12 year old, heading into seventh grade.

My table set took a day to refinish. The deck took three days. The sunroom took three weeks. We're past our second-year mark and have officially headed into our third. Our patience is worn and thin, but our hope has proven to be the most resilient. Each day is another step toward recovery. Rehabilitation is a necessary part of that recovery and one we accept. It takes a lot of strength every day not to fall into sadness and anxiety over this process. Trying to make life as normal as possible for Drew, Kevin and Ryan helps us keep focus. Life is full of renovations and there's always some work that needs to be done. Our foundations may need support and the walls a fresh coat of paint. If only Drew's renovations were that easy.

"We are pressed on every side by troubles, but we are not crushed and broken. We are perplexed, but we don't give up and quit." 2 Corinthians 4:8 (NIV)

Wishing you all a wonderful July,
Team D'Auteuil

Chapter 46

"How great the dignity of the soul, since each one has from his birth an angel commissioned to guard it." – St. Jerome, 4th century (New Advent Catholic Encyclopedia)

When Kevin and Ryan were born, my mother gave them a prayer card. It remains on their dresser to this day. *"Angel of God, my guardian dear to whom God's love commits me here. Ever this day, or night, be at my side to light and guard, to rule and guide. Amen."* I think when many of us hear the word "angel," we conjure up images of ethereal, gauzy beauty in a human form with wings and a halo. The English word "angel" comes from the Greek angelos, which means "messenger." The bible is full of passages about angels, their human forms, their appearances and the messages they bring. Since I was old enough to attend church, I learned about angels. Angels have been mentioned in the Old Testament and the New Testament, even before the time of Christ. Hollywood has altered and adjusted angels to more contemporary images of tall, handsome men in suits or beautiful women, mingling with the rest of us undetected. We use the adjective "angelic" to describe babies and have called people an "angel" when they have helped us with a problem. We had met several "angels" on this journey and feel blessed to have had them enter our lives during this difficult time. If you were to ask me, "do I believe in angels?", I would have to answer "yes," for I have already met several.

I obviously use that term to describe people who have touched my life in a very real, very human way during this unwelcome journey. I have mentioned them all during this story. At this time, I can say truthfully that I believe that there was an intervention either by, on or behalf of God. By estimate, there were probably hundreds of people praying for Drew that awful week of April 11th , 2010. I believe that God heard those prayers and answered.

In September 2008, Time Magazine printed an article about angels. *"More than half of all Americans believe they have been helped by a guardian angel in the course of their lives, according to a new poll by the Baylor University Institute for Studies of Religion. In a poll of 1700 respondents, 55% answered affirmatively to the statement, "I was protected from harm by a guardian angel." The responses defied standard class and denominational assumptions about religious belief; the majority held up regardless of denomination, region or education — though the figure was a little lower (37%) among respondents earning more than $150,000 a year."*

That poll was a pleasant surprise to me, considering how increasingly secular the world is becoming. Drew's journey has its personal meaning for me as I unabashedly and completely relied on God to carry me, if not all of us, through this. My mother's favorite saying during times of trouble was "put it in God's hands." God gave mankind free will. We cannot and should not expect him to intervene. But he did…he did intervene and Drew is living proof. I believe with all my heart that our life, leading up to Drew's diagnosis and thereinafter, clearly shows the hand of God at every painful twist and turn. I see that there was a reason for where we lived, the people we knew, people we would meet and the events in April 2010 that showed his wondrous intervention for Drew. I remember Drew, telling me about "Nana" when he never met her, and wonder again about angels among us. Was that a pre-emptive visit? Was Drew visited by someone when he was three years old, or was it just the imaginative babbling of an adorable preschooler? Does he have a guardian angel? God only knows.

The existence of angels is a defined actuality of the catholic faith (**Catechism of the Catholic Church 328**), but the concept of the guardian angel and its role is not clearly defined and continues to be discussed and debated to this day. St. Thomas Aquinas stated that *"(1.) God sends angels to minister to his purposes among bodily creatures……When God has an angel apply its powers to a creature, the angel is sent to that creature. God is the sender and the first principle of the effect produced by the angel sent; God is also the ultimate goal or final cause of the work so produced. The angel is God's minister or intelligent instrument; by its being sent it renders ministry to God."* Angels are not defined or described in the bible as humans who have passed away. *"The angels are represented throughout the Bible as a body of spiritual beings intermediate between God and men: "You have made him (man) a little less than the angels"* (Psalm 8:6).

St. Thomas Aquinas further goes on to say that *"(6.) The guardian angel is a gift of divine providence. He never fails or forsakes his charge. Sometimes, in the workings of providence, a man must suffer trouble; this is not prevented by the guardian angel."* Drew had a terrible illness - a death sentence without treatment, but that treatment had its own risks and complications. I look back at the worst times. Four times of intensive worry about Drew's health, especially April 2010, and see intervention just when we reached the peak of desperation and anxiety about what would happen next. Twice his gallbladder brought him to the point of danger and then spontaneously resolved. Drew's extraordinary and rapid recovery in April 2010 and again in July 2010. No doubt in my mind God's work, complementing the phenomenal medical care he received.

I do believe that God knew Drew was going to get sick and He guided our life in a way to support us the best, including the best doctors. When even those doctors couldn't save him, He stepped in. Whether that gift of healing was delivered by an angel or God, didn't matter to me. What mattered to me was that I *believed*. It took six months of encouraging for me to write this book. To write it meant I had to accept it. To accept it, I have to believe. I do believe. I believe in God and I believe in miracles. The answer that I was looking for through Drew's illness, his miraculous recovery and writing this book is that *I believe*. I don't *need* to know why or how. I just have to believe.

Chapter 47

In November of 2009, free will, kindness and generosity led Steven Manro to drive 250 miles away from home in Germany to donate his life-saving bone marrow to our son. Steven didn't know where his marrow was going, or to whom it would be given. He chose to do it of his own free will. On November 18th, 2009, Drew received the gift that allowed him to defeat aplastic anemia.

It was a wonderful day on March 24th, 2012, when we were privileged to speak to Steven on the phone. To attempt to tell him in words how grateful we were felt inadequate and minimal. Steven just wanted to know how Drew was doing and seemed genuinely happy to talk to him. Steven told us that he joined the registry when he learned that there was a local boy in a neighboring town who needed a bone marrow transplant. He told us how happy he was that he was called as a match, and that he didn't hesitate, or even have to think about it. To Steven, it was simply the right thing to do. For that, we'll always be grateful.

Since that day, we have emailed and shared photos. Someday, we hope to thank him in person and allow Drew to meet his blood brother. Until that time, we are connected by his generous gift of life that flows through Drew. Not a day goes by that I don't think about him and thank God that Steven was a match and that he was willing to share that gift of life for Drew.

Epilogue

Drew continues to regain his strength and reclaim the life of a normal boy that he was denied for so long. He has faced numerous challenges such as graft vs. host disease, high blood pressure and kidney damage. His full recovery will likely be long term. We are all so grateful for the care he receives from Alli and everyone at the Jimmy Fund and Children's Hospital Boston. I don't ask anymore why or how Drew defied the odds. We know that Drew was given the gift of a second chance, in reality more than once, during this journey.

This is where faith comes in. Faith is believing without proof. Faith is accepting God's will, no matter how hard it seems. At times when we thought we would be angry or resentful for what our family was going through, we instead looked to our faith for strength to see us through it. Believing in something so powerful was easy. That's not to say that it was always easy. Having faith is the *easy* part...accepting what will be is the tough part. Faith is believing that God hears you. Faith is knowing that God is present every day in our lives, not just the times we need him the most. If we have faith, we believe that God walks beside us and when life doesn't go the way we hoped or planned, it's faith that leads us to lean on His strength to help us cope.

We also look at how our life was organized at the time as if we were somehow unconsciously prepared for this journey. We had paid off all debt including our cars. We had decided not to incur tuition charges by keeping our sons in the town high school. We had our friends, the Nelsons, who had already been down this road, to rely on for support. Pete had a job that offered flexibility with time off and a flight department of fellow pilots who kept him covered, for many months while Drew was going through his transplant. We belonged to a church and lived in a town where we were enveloped by generous, supportive people. We were surrounded by local organizations and businesses that supported us. Even the shop owner, Ross, who cut the boys' hair, lived right up the street from us.

We also believe that our faith was reinforced by witnessing the astonishing courage of a young boy, the strength of his brothers and the lifesaving generosity of a complete stranger, half a world away. How can you not believe in God when there are people like this and doctors who have been given gifts and talent to help families like ours?

Drew is no longer struggling to face his physical limitations, rather those limitations are challenged by his seemingly limitless ability to defy the odds. He still has challenges ahead to face and I will always pray for his continued strength, courage and resilience. He was 10 years old when this journey started and is now emerging as a teenager who just wants to be normal and still may not have a clear understanding of just what a miracle his mere presence in the world is. Drew may also never understand the inspiration that his illness and recovery gave to so many who followed his journey. I never thought that my son's illness and writing a blog about it would provide such a network of love, support and prayers that I would eventually come to depend on. I didn't realize until now how therapeutic writing about this journey would be and how it would enable me to look back and see so clearly the message I was looking for.

As we didn't know, all those years ago, the direction our lives would turn, we do not know what the future holds. We no longer look for an explanation as to why our son had to go through this, rather the message that our journey offers. We will rely on our faith to help us keep the perspective that this life-altering event has given us. We can and we will be happy again. We will thank God every day for the grace that helped us through the past few years and continues to guide us. We will thank God for the kindness that was shown to us and use that to help guide our actions when we see others in need. We have so much to be thankful. Most of all, we will thank God for the miracle that occurred in April 2010 and will never forget that our prayers were answered.

There are some who might debate that coincidence or chance, in addition to the superior medical care he received, is to be solely credited with Drew's miraculous recovery. Free will gives you the option of believing whatever you want. After all, God's greatest gift to man was free will. This is our story and what we believe. Drew had the greatest medical care available. But in April 2010, even that wasn't enough. I have been convinced, and have living proof, that medical science and faith can co-exist. His name is Drew. There's no reason for faith and medicine to be mutually exclusive. We had the best of the best caring for Drew *and* we also believed. If reading our story affirms your faith and makes you believe in miracles, then the message of Drew's journey has been delivered. You just have to decide to receive it.

As for me, I'll continue to write in Drew's blog as the inspiration comes to me or when I have news to share. I'll continue my newfound endeavor to promote awareness of AA and advocate fiercely for the bone marrow registry. I will also never stop believing in miracles and guardian angels. As for my next book...well, I'm leaning toward a comedy.

"Do not be anxious about anything, but in every situation, by prayer and petition, with thanksgiving, present your requests to God." **Philippians 4:6 (NIV)**

Photo courtesy of Rick Lopez Photography

Drew, longstick defender on right, Lacrosse spring 2012.

Portion of proceeds going toward, but not limited to:
Jimmy Fund Pediatric SCT/BMT Research
Children's Hospital Boston 6th floor parking and pizza funds
Joe Andruzzi Foundation
Make A Wish Foundation NH
Children's Hospital at Dartmouth
Jaiden's Angel Foundation
Partners in Health - Nashua
Hole in the Wall Gang
St. Jude's Children's Hospital
CaringBridge.org and Care Pages
Dream Day on the Cape Foundation
Motivating Miles Foundation
AA/MDS Foundation

Van Biema, David, (September 2008). Guardian Angels are Here, Say Most Americans. *Time Magazine*. Retrieved from www.time.com/time/nation/article/0,8599,1842179,00.html.

Existence of Angels. *Catechism of the Catholic Church, 2nd Ed. Part I: The Profession of Faith*. 328. Retrieved from www.scborromeo.org/ccc/p1s2c1p5.htm

Msng Paul J. Glenn. Summa Theologica Ia. *A Tour of the Summa. The First Part*, Questions 106-114. (teachings of St. Thomas Aquinas) Retrieved from http://www.jesus-passion.com/angels.htm

CPSIA information can be obtained at www.ICGtesting.com
Printed in the USA
BVOW021601071212

307519BV00002B/154/P